Women Speak

VOLUME TEN

Edited by Kari Gunter-Seymour

Story~Poetry~Song

ISBN: 978-1-962405-10-2
Sheila-Na-Gig Editions
Russel, Kentucky
www.sheilanagigblog.com

EDITOR: Kari Gunter-Seymour
LINE EDITOR: Hayley Mitchell Haugan
COVER DESIGN: Kari Gunter-Seymour
COVER ART: Marlene L'Abbe

INQUIRIES:
Kari Gunter-Seymour, Executive Director
womenofappalachia@gmail.com
www.womenofappalachia.com
FACEBOOK: Women of Appalachia Project

Women Speak

VOLUME TEN

CONTENTS

DEDICATION:

The Women of Appalachia Project
wishes to dedicate this issue to the many courageous survivors
of Hurricane Helene and in remembrance of all
who were torn from us.

By and by, Lord, By and by...

Monic Ductan

Confederate

At the bridge's underbelly stands a woman,
Thin jacket shielding her from pelting sleet.
A worse sight in this town I've scarcely seen—
Her slouching there, broken hat brim
Covering parts of her matted, blonde hair.
Her fingers, in their tattered gloves, hold a sign:
"Homeless at X-Mas." She's ageless,
Not because she's aged well, but because
I cannot place her age. I'd think her an old woman
If not for the spry gait that brings her
To my car window. Ignoring my boyfriend's sigh,
I dig the few dollars from the cup holder,
Press the bills to her brown-gloved palm,
Which matches my own dark skin.
My boyfriend stares at something I cannot see
Until we pull forward. The beggar woman
Mounts a bike, a Confederate flag on one handlebar,
A MAGA flag on the other. As I let my car idle
There under the bridge, the cars behind me honk
Like a dozen trumpets out of tune.
Traffic shakes everything—the icy pavement,
The very air whooshing in through the open window.
A line of cars ahead of us winds through the sleet,
Up and up, toward the foggy mountains.

Monic Ductan

Homer, Georgia

I want to be fourteen again. Singing
"Come On Up to Bright Glory"
In a robed church choir. Swaying
Shoulder to shoulder with round black women
Who smell like Dentyne and cocoa butter.
Long afternoons passed in the church basement
Eating macaroni casserole, cornbread,
And Kool-Aid with a curly-haired boy I like.
The boy asked me to walk with him outside.
We crept over the gravel lot and turned
To the graveyard. Tombstones overgrown
And peppered with dandelions. We moved
Farther down the row, passed older graves
Of people who perhaps used to walk this field
With sweethearts who held their hands and whispered.
I wore my grown-up sandals, two inches tall.
How strange it was to think of kissing
While standing so close to Granddaddy's grave.
Imagining his bones beneath our feet. Seeing
Patches of grass newly smooshed by my heels.
Touching this boy's hair, not understanding
How to tilt my head when his face is suddenly
In front of me. His nose bumps mine.
Bump. Bump. Bump. Separating our lips.

I saw him recently, that boy, who is bald now,
And for a moment I understand nostalgia,
This longing for a thing that no longer exists.
Yesterday, in search of that church,
I drove down 198. But there was no gravel lot,
No clapboard, no white paint. I'm *sure*

It must be *there*. But I saw only dense woods
And a country road, smelled pine trees in fresh air.
I should have stopped and walked those acres
To search for the graveyard. To spend some time
With Granddaddy and Grandmama.
For a moment, my memories were less real
Because I could not find the burial places.
Where I walked and I sang, was held underwater
By an old country preacher now long dead. I want
To turn this car around. But I keep going
Into a part of the county I haven't seen. Gasping,
Searching for something familiar. Gasping,
Like coming up for air after a long, deep kiss.

Monic Ductan

Being Pampered by My Five-Year-Old

He likes to touch my hair at the roots,
To rub the wavy places.
He counts the grey hairs aloud.
When he gets to ten,
I tell him to pull them out.
He grabs a fistful of hair,
Tugs like he's opening a stuck door.
When I squeal, he says,
Sorry. I didn't mean to hurted you.

He admires the nail polish on my dresser,
Rolls the bottles across the carpet—
Pink fantasy, blue bonnet, teal dream.
He paints my nails in alternating colors,
The paint bunching around the cuticles,
Spots of blue bleeding into my skin.
He holds my hand up to the light,
Says, *Now it's a beauty.*

I marvel at this boy who puts his dolls to bed
Under folded blankets, drops wet kisses
On their plastic cheeks. He links
The dolls' stiff hands together,
So they won't be lonely in the dark.
How will he navigate this world?
Will he be coerced into strapping on a helmet,
Tackling? Belching through tailgate parties,
Striding tall, leading with his crotch?

I once witnessed a boy teased for rubbing
His girlfriend's cheek. I wish
My son to be that boy, to have a pliant heart,
Capable of expanding like a balloon.
Will he become a man who gives foot rubs
To every woman whose scent rests on his sheets?
Lordy mercy, I hope so.

Connie Jordan Green

Holy Weeds

It satisfies my soul the way a root
lets go in moist soil, the way a weed—
lambs quarter, smartweed, chickweed—
comes up whole in my hand, stem intact,
a map of roots dangling beyond my wrist,
fresh earth aroma and the scent of green
the incense I inhale, the way weeding sanctifies
a row of beans, makes perfect the corn stalks
marching through the garden. By morning
the first verdant tips—unrepentant sinners—
populate the cathedral, dispute the ritual of row
and pathway, the holy order labor imposed, forgiveness
no part of this liturgy, only more hours on my knees,
obeisance to the profligate spirit that rules all life.

Connie Jordan Green

Where Poetry Comes From

At the edge of a turquoise
        sea is a cave filled
                with hieroglyphics

and the secret faces
        of bats, and in the sea
                are dolphins with minds

beyond the comprehension
        of humans, and far out
                in the sea are whales.

All night the whales
        rise with their magnificent
                blowholes,

and they call out to the stars
        and to the planets lined
                in the summer sky

like the lines of a sonnet,
        and all of language rests
                where whale and dolphin

spend their innumerable days,
        and where bats wait for dark,
                and the cave breathes its cool air.

Connie Jordan Green

After a Year of Grief

When the sun slips lower and lower
on the horizon, and the corners
in your kitchen remain dark day
after day, when night comes too fast
and lasts too long, and you can
scarcely raise your arms to lift
your youngest child, then comes
a day you glimpse the self
you used to be, a quick glance
as she vanishes around the corner.
You take out your broom,
your dust cloth, and slowly you
clean one room and then another,
the shadow of your former self
lengthening with each sweep
of the broom. You raise your head,
gaze out upon the familiar pasture
rolling away down the hill
as it always has done, and you
remember how in summer it will be
filled with clover and bees, how
yellow light will spread across
the stoop as if all you need do
is step over the threshold.

Jacinda Townsend

Fences

-an excerpt from Trigger Warning

Ruth had said she'd be waiting for him in the parking lot, and she was, sitting on the trunk of her Tesla, oblivious to his arrival. Myron got out of his car and studied the back of her head, the tight, neat French braid she'd put there. Her hair was more carroty, even, than Enix's; when he'd first met her, he'd looked for the statistically likely lone brown strand per fifty and found none. Ruth had never been able to tolerate sunlight, which had been a joke among their White friends in college. There had been Ruth, smearing SPF50, buying sombreros at beaches. After college, when they were first living together and then married, she locked the front door in broad daylight. She set the emergency brake in her car even when she was just parking in their driveway.

All of it—all of Ruth's secret and unpredictable foci—had grated on Myron during their marriage. Now, with some distance, he saw that she hadn't meant him any harm: fever was just her way. If it could be said that everyone on earth was secretly fighting a battle inside, Ruth was fighting five thousand. She couldn't be helped, and it had taken him all these years to realize. He saw her, from behind and then, as he approached, from the side, saw she had her thousand-dollar Canon strapped across her chest. He saw her as she saw him, a man now unneeded, a prong who no longer fit any outlet in her soul. She wore a sharp, dark lipstick he'd never seen, and a walnut suede skirt that matched the darker glaze she'd put over her blaze of hair.

She looked down and fiddled with her camera's telegraphic lens, her elbows bowed out from her body as wings from a delicate moth. He'd never wanted her as badly when they were married as he wanted her now.

He got closer. Tapped her on the shoulder. "Hey," he said.

She did not rise. "Annie has homework this weekend," she said, wearily.

He felt his shoulders hunching into the childhood version of himself, which was the model he most hated. He'd been a cowed, rotten boy who'd watched an LDS missionary singe the fur off a cat's paws, repeatedly, and said nothing. The cat had ignored the flame initially, and then, as his fur thinned, yelped in pain, and still, Myron had simply stood next to his own bicycle and watched. Had he grown apart from that version of himself, he wondered, or had the self simply grown into him, inner rings of a tree? He couldn't now say.

Ruth picked up the camera, took aim at him, rotated her lens. Dropped the camera's body back to her chest. "Have a good time," she said. "I'll pick her up Sunday."

Myron nodded. If he opened his mouth, or even just his throat, to murmur assent, he'd open some seventh seal of misery that would pour out and flood the world.

The final straw between them had been a piece of bullshit having to do with his computer password. It was a joke that wasn't funny, one he never should have put on his laptop in the first place. But he knew that there were deeper issues, ones Ruth was simply refusing to disclose. He was so small in his lack of self-insight, he supposed, she hadn't deigned to offer him truth. She'd simply filed, and in typical Ruth fashion, never looked back.

She'd been the one to plant all her belongings in a giant U-Haul and flee the family home, but not before asking for it back. From her new luxury apartment in East Louisville, she filed motions for her promise of half his pension. She wanted alimony. She wanted sole decision-making power over Enix's educational future. His lawyer, upon reading her initial petition aloud to Myron, had nicknamed her The Bulldog.

Myron made an exercise now of remembering her as she was in their first little house, the one they rented right after they got married, the single-story bungalow she filled with plants and more plants. She'd started out with a huge cactus on the front porch, almost as caricature, but then she'd filled the front yard with cacti, and added rhododendron and dragon trees. She put a towering ficus in the corner of their living room near the television, and a chili pepper plant on the kitchen windowsill. She put small, square pots of thyme and sage on the porch columns.

After Annie was born, she filled the backyard, and she filled Annie's nursery, even, with greenery, and it seemed that every time Annie napped, Ruth spent the hour or two tending her various gardens rather than talking tohim. Finally, there came the day when he yelled out to her to put down her watering jug and come in—*hurry!*—because PBS was rerunning *The Black Power Mixtape.*

"Plants won't water themselves," she'd yelled back in at him.

He heard this for the ruse it was. Ruth had always eschewed the political, refusing to attend college anti-apartheid rallies with him, waving voter registration volunteers out of her way when they approached on street corners. She didn't seem to understand this part of Blackness, though he'd come to find this flaw as endearing as it was regrettable. But the tone. Her tone. It was the tone that had made him ask, "Why are you turning this house into a fucking arboretum, anyway?"

He heard the plastic clatter as the watering jug fell to the porch. She came and stood in the open back door. Her neck had turned red. "I just want to nurture something that's not pooping or screaming at me," she said. Her nose turned red and she started crying, sobbing in big gulps of air. "I want to raise something that's not going to have to have therapy later because I looked at it the wrong way. Is that okay with you, Sir Myron?"

"I'm sorry," he told her. "I didn't mean to hurt your feelings."

"What feelings. I don't have feelings anymore. There isn't time."

As Annie had grown, Ruth had let the plants, one by one, wither and die, and when she and Myron left the rented house and moved into their own, they had only to take with them the old front porch cactus that had been the original plant. In those five years Ruth had somehow transferred her neuroses cleanly and neatly into parenting, which is why Myron wasn't surprised when she said, now, "I need to know what time to pick Enix up on Sunday. I mean exactly. It's what all the divorce books say. You need to give me an exact time."

"What—is Enix performing surgery?"

"Good fences make good neighbors," she said. She was still seated on the trunk of her car, which made her taller than him. It felt like some sort of power move. She scratched the end of her nose with the heel of her hand. She didn't give a shit about his feelings. It was possible she never had.

He winced. Visibly and, he hoped, purposefully. "Fine. I mean, here's a day of the week when no one has anywhere to be, but whatever. How about 3:00?"

"That's so late to be starting homework."

"I can supervise homework. It's still in my job description."

Ruth transmitted a look of catlike satisfaction. "Thank you," she said. "Her math book's in her bag."

Annie's backpack, blue with its purple Tecumseh camp logo, was on the ground beside the car, and he hoisted it over his shoulder, then bent down and picked up her clarinet case. She was first chair clarinet this year and had finagled her way into playing a solo at the eighth-grade graduation.

"Enix," he said now, for they'd descended from the passenger seat of their mother's car with the army jacket around their shoulders and dog tags swinging, signaling their return to manliness. Enix turned their face to the sky, closed their eyes as if to shut out their parents. Ruth came in for a hug but Enix held stiff against the goodbye, their arms limp at their sides. "Go, Mom," they said. Their neck was turning red. "See you Sunday."

Days earlier, Myron had made an appointment with his lawyer, Melani Sutton, and now, on his way downtown, he cracked the car windows to let in the pollinated spring. The unusually fierce winter had worn their minds to thread but now, driving down Brownsboro towards 71S, he could smell the promise of honeysuckle. He remembered himself as a kid, pulling the flower's stigma to suck nectar from the middle. He was so far from that now. He was a man growing old, trimming his ear hair, losing his sense of smell, drying out of testosterone.

He'd heard from Melani that morning—Ruth was rejecting his settlement offer. She should have been especially agitated when they met up to transfer Enix, but she hadn't been. True, the relative quiet of the pandemic and its aftermath had thrown cover over the small, frenetic bird in Ruth's mind. But her calm made him wonder what she knew that he didn't. She'd always held, in the tuck of her elbow, in the set of her mouth, a certain ether of unoffered information; she was a chambered nautilus of mystery. She had a line of freckles under one eye that made her look, perpetually, as if she'd been crying, and when she answered his deeper questions—did she miss her dead mother, was she devastated that Enix was failing World Science—she'd roll off casual responses that made him unable to decide what she wasn't telling him.

The only thing she'd told him about her past was that when she was six years old, her parents had died, entwined together on a cold, sticky floor, on their way out of the Hollywood Supper Club Fire. Myron had vaguely remembered the huge tragedy: 165 dead. But as Ruth relayed her parents' singular story to him, just a community college janitor and a housewife out for a rare night on the town, what had been a major news story even turned Technicolor real in his head. "Dad used to be the last person in every building," she'd told him. "It was so spooky to watch, the way he had to shut off all the lights until he got to the one that would let him see his way out the door. And then, for him and Mom to die like that? In perfect darkness? Well."

Ruth had told him how the four of her grandparents had collected her parents' charred bodies, the way she then bounced between the two sets of them, Baileys on school nights, Carrs on the weekends. Really, she said, when she saw his eyes widen, it was an unremarkable childhood. She sipped her Stella, and Myron felt himself continuing to stare at her. She felt it, too. She shrugged her shoulders and looked off into space.

The next day he'd sat outside her dorm room for hours, hoping to casually run into her on her way to the shower. She'd be shrouded in towels, he knew, but the prospect of her nakedness wasn't the point. He wanted to experience the raw, magnetic truth of her, her bare feet, her wet hair. He didn't love her, necessarily, but he respected her presence in a way that frightened him. "What are you doing here, you creep," a young woman had finally said, in passing, and he left the hall. But it was a disappointment. Ruth moved in a space of puzzlement she'd never let him crack, so he married it. Hoping one day to be close enough, he could break in and burglarize.

He hadn't. And now, Melani Sutton was telling him, he would not. He could scratch Ruth off his bucket list. They were in Melani's office, at her law firm, which was so close to his own, in a fifteen-story building that clotted the sun from the street below. Myron situated Enix and her things in a chair in the outer hall then followed the working lights of the trail of recessed ceiling bars leading to Melani's door.

"Howdy," she said. "Have a seat."

He wheeled his chair closer to her door before sitting, so he could still look down the hall and watch Enix, who was now fingering the shiny metal keys of their clarinet. He watched the light trained on the crown of his kid's head, how it set aflame the orange highlights in their auburn hair. Enix arched their fingers to hold a long whole note before flying through a crescendo of sixteenths, and Myron felt a prod of resentment against their musicianship, their ability to float so far above the cloying world, trailing thirty-second notes and fermatas behind them.

"This is all pretty standard," Melani was saying. Her voice was unnaturally high. A cartoon voice, a voice on helium. "And I don't know how you'll feel about this, but she's changing her name back to Cottam."

"Cottam?"

"Cottam."

He didn't understand. He'd married a Ruth Bailey. Ruth Elizabeth Bailey, he thought he'd married, but now, even her middle name wasn't holding still. It was in twelve-point font, three paragraphs down a sheet of paper Melani was sliding toward him: Ruth Louise Cottam.

"Her maiden name," Melani said slowly, as if they were no longer speaking English. He needed to relieve his bladder, but he was the client this time, pinned in place.

"Cottam?" he asked again, this time with sourness, and Melani cocked her head, stared into his eyes. She was assessing his pupils, he knew. He couldn't bear to look back at her, and instead watched as the air conditioning trapped one wiry strand of her hair in its current.

Randi Ward

Nest

Never
regret
being
empty,
never
expect
to be
let
down
gently.

Randi Ward

Walking Stick

I'm sorry
I pretend
not to
lean
on you
as much
as I do.

Christina Fisanick

Where I'm From

I am from the bottom of Chicken Neck Hill
where we bake our pizza in squares
and pile fried fish high on white bread.

I am from winding roads and rolling hills
where the symphony plays under firework skies.

I am from lake shores and mud bogs
and have more than one pair of crick shoes
for catching minnows and crawdads
that my rich friends like to call crayfish.

I am from Walter Reuther and Mother Jones.
Red bandanas and picket signs.
I am from swinging axes and shoveling coal.
From company stores and shotgun shacks.

I am from lightning bugs signaling summer's arrival
and streetlights telling me it's time to go home.
I am from backyard fires and moonshine stills.
Burnt-black marshmallows and cicada song.

I am from the "Gateway to the West,"
where wagon trains lumbered along National Road
and steamboats floated to New Orleans
down the rambling Ohio.

I am from the Fish Crick deal and going alone.
And too much coffee and not enough smokes.

I am from eating tomatoes warm off their vines,
secret ramp patches deep in the woods,
and walnut-stained hands after the first hard frost.

I am from hollers and valleys and old pickup trucks.
I am from hillsides blazing with color on Sunday drives
and porch sitting with neighbors in the nowhere of dusk.

I am from hands that hurt and hands that heal,
and I am stronger than pig iron forged into steel.

Stephanie Kendrick

Sun Tea

My mother used her fill of the sun—
slathered herself with Coppertone,
splayed on a faded towel bought
with Marlboro Miles. She siphoned
the rays with the will of a woman
who ignored warning labels as much
as she ignored the sweat bees swarming halos
around her dew-slicked forehead.

Near her on the grass, a large Mason jar,
three tea bags, a sliver of bark,
handful of clover buds.
At the color of honey, she added sugar.
At the color of her skin,
it was ready to taste.

The way she stayed in that same bikini for days,
a cloud of coconut aroma following her
as she rolled onto her chiseled hip
toward the jar—the way she held the sides
with her small hands, gently swished
the settled sweetness—
the way she tipped it to Revlon lips,
left a smudge on the rim,
smiled as she poured a smaller jar for me—

this is how I learned
to worship.

Stephanie Kendrick

In the age of Cancer

humans cherished mothers—worshipped them. I am a Cancer. Born under a summer moon beginning to rise, I entered the world tasting my mother's sweat and joining her in scream. Neither of us ever quite mastered melody but rage rested in our bodies like a guard dog, never completely reposed. Under another summer moon, on a Monday, a doctor saw my mother's tumor on a screen and he said the word, "tumor" and I left my body for a moment and squinted for outcomes like stars, trying to make shapes that I could name. She had rid her body of Cancer before—I was there—I still feel the quake of her purge, consider the other parasites she expelled and I think of her body, all it has conquered and loved. In the age of Cancer humans began building homes, and I am a Cancer and her body was my home until her body cast me out and I cried for the first time while she cried and when the doctor said "tumor" I left my body for a moment—tried to find my way back to hers.

every birthday
I will send screams to the moon
they are meant for her

Tina Parker

The Signs

Dress me in sackcloth
Pluck the hairs from my head
Loose the serpent
Let it wind
Around my body
Hold a flame to my chin
Pour the strychnine
Pass me a cup
Lay hands on me
That I may be healed.

Tina Parker

The Viewing

My dad was laid out so pretty
My mom went on about what a good job
The barber had done with his hair
Pleased she'd had the wherewithal
To take him for a trim the week before
He could walk until he couldn't

Then we viewed him in his first casket
His recliner
I sat with him nights
Said the *shh shh* (prayer) hand to forehead
To calm him dosed the morphine
I did not run away though my instinct
Was to curl up at my mother's side

My mom declared his second casket
Far more beautiful than she recalled
He wore his glasses held a white handkerchief
My brother placed a small Bible from childhood
I did not add the *uh-uh-uh* sound
He made (his pain)
I did not add the songs I sang
Or the nights I kept vigil
I did not crawl in and curl at his side.

Tina Parker

Deep Shade

The holler at dusky dark
Train tracks by the creek
Your mama pouring honey over biscuits
The sweetness that makes you want more

Train whistle
Coal hopper comes off #6 full
You close your eyes
A warm hand presses to your forehead
A prayer
Shh shh, I got you

A light far off blinks
Through the dark
Your daddy's mining hat
Laughter
Cigarette smoke
Your brothers and sisters
Talking and carrying on
Into the night

You are aloft weightless
Held by so many hands
The crowd carries you
Lifts you up to the angel band

Organ hymn handbells
The mountains open
To a great green valley
White flick of a deer's tail
The whoosh of wings
A heron takes flight.

Alexis T. Nichols

Cornishville

Cornishville is a town that used to be. Before I knew it, there used to be a post office, a firehouse, and a gas station. There used to be big, black tobacco barns, hardy Duroc hogs flopping around in mudholes, and an old mill that ran the whole town on the rush of the Chaplin River. There used to be church ladies batting away at mosquitoes from their screen doors, young boys casting their lines off the bridge over the waterfall, and cakewalks in the Fellowship Hall. There used to be little children bounding towards each other while playing Red Rover, panting in the sweltry heat of the valley like the wandering cemetery dog they pet on. Cornishville used to be alive no matter how little there was. I know it, because I was alive there for a while.

Cornishville used to be a whole lot of things, but it isn't much of anything now. People keep calling it a ghost town, nothing but druggies and fighting people and old people who can't move on. Truth be told, I reckon most people born there left in a way they can't ever come back from, and the only time they'd want to anyhow would be to lay a bouquet of plastic flowers on a headstone or spread sod over a grave. Even then, the drive down there will make their babies carsick, and that's a good enough excuse as any to stay away.

People keep calling it a ghost town, and I keep wanting to haul off and hit them. So, I guess that makes me one of them old biddies who can't move on. And I reckon my family are them druggies and fighting people, no matter how hard they worked to clean up our name. But I remember Cornishville in the rich crumbles of potato candy, the waxy pears in my Christmas stocking, and the static hiss of sparklers. I remember it in the red flocking of the church pews and the sycamores that swayed over the river. I remember it in the people who laughed because they didn't have to worry so long as Jesus was watching.

Natalie Sypolt

Summer Theme

"If I had a car," Gina thought for the hundredth time, "Things would be different."

Depending on people was one of the hardest things. She hated asking for rides, and she'd rather walk and hitch if she could. Somehow hitching didn't feel like asking. You just walk, and if someone wants to stop and pick you up, they do; there's no obligation and no uncomfortable moment where you both know that they want to say no, but that they won't because they feel sorry for you. Gina doesn't want anyone, ever, to feel sorry for her.

After school, Gina worked register at the Dollar General, which was close to school, but kind of far from her house. It wasn't a bad walk to work, but at night she hated to walk home. She had nearly gotten hit so many times that she bought those little stick-on reflectors and attached them to the back of her jacket.

On Mondays and Wednesdays, Bob McGraw, the store manager, would give her a ride home. He was a grandfather and she thought he was safe until he started sliding his hand across the console towards her leg, and she realized that men of all ages are just about the same.

"Hey Gina," someone called as she walked down the steps of the high school. "Gina!" She turned around to see Brandon coming toward her, smiling in that movie star way. He was so good looking that he was almost ugly, like almost not really possible. He did not talk to Gina, not since the fourth grade when kids started figuring out who was necessary and who was not. They'd been lunch friends before that, but she was most definitely in the not category.

"Yeah?" she said, turning to look at him, but not stopping.

"Wait up a minute." He jogged towards her, his brown hair a bouncing, healthy wave.

"What?" Gina barked, sounding harsher than she intended, and she saw Brandon stop short.

"Um, I just wondered if you wanted a ride home? I always see you walking, and I think I go right past where you live so I could give you a ride if you want?" He sounded so unsure, every statement ending in a question mark. Gina was a little charmed in spite of herself but knew there was a catch. There was always a catch, and people like

Brandon didn't offer things to people like her.

"I'm going to work," she said.

"Oh, over at the DG, right?" he said, using the abbreviation that made Gina's teeth clench. She knew it was a way to make fun of the store, ironically making it sound cool because it was anything but. "I go by there too. Want a ride?"

Gina narrowed her eyes. Her brain told her to run away and her body noticed that he had taken a step closer. He was taller than her by at least a head and smelled like something clean, like soap and licorice.

"No," she said.

He must have heard the hesitation in her voice, saw a small opening, because he smiled wider and said, "Oh, come on."

His car wasn't old or new, but somewhere in between. Probably a hand me down from his parents. It was nice, but not too nice. Clean, but not too clean. Perfectly beige.

With Brandon, Gina didn't have to worry about thinking of things to say, because he talked. A lot. That first drive from school to work, he talked for the whole fifteen minutes. She was afraid he was going to ask her questions, all the things they all wondered about her, but he just jabbered on and on about his Chem class and how the teacher was out on maternity leave but had recorded all these lectures so, it was like learning Chemistry from the disembodied voice of God. In a weird way, it was relaxing, and she liked watching him drive. He was confident, but also very careful and came to full stops at all the stop signs.

...

For the next two weeks, Brandon waited for her outside of school and drove her to work. She never presumed, never met him at his car. For the fifteen-minute drive, he would talk about what ever bullshit thing was going on and she would listen, first pressed hard against the door, but then relaxing as he didn't reach over the center console to touch her.

One night, she was walking home after work. It was dark and starting to rain, and a car pulled up next to her. She turned and saw Brandon's nondescript beige car behind her, catching her in the headlights.

"Get in, stupid," he shouted out the window. She went to the passenger side and fell into the seat, happy for the refuge from the weather. Brandon shook his head at her and started driving her home after work.

If there was whispering about her and Brandon, she didn't hear it above all the other whispering. Gina was the girl who had been pregnant and had come to school with t-shirts pulled tight across her big belly and no maternity clothes. Then she was the girl who wasn't pregnant anymore, but there was also no baby because she'd given it away. Or it was taken away. Maybe she killed it even and put it in a trash can like those girls you hear about.

Most everybody took a wide swing around Gina, like her disease was one that was catching.

"So listen," Brandon said one night as he drove her home. The days were staying light longer as it neared summer, and the sky was a dark sunset, green and murky looking except for slashes of orange and pink. That color made the inside of the car look smoldering. "Don't say no."

Gina took a deep breath. This was going to be it, the other shoe was finally going to come down on her throat.

"There is a party—"

"No," she said quickly.

"I said don't say no!" Brandon hit the brakes, suddenly stopping them right in the middle of the road. No cars were coming behind them, but there could be one any minute and Gina felt desperate for him to move. "There is an end of year party out at Maggie Jenson's pool. There's going to be a bonfire and stuff. It'll be fun."

"No," Gina said again and looked in her mirror. If someone came flying up behind them, they'd probably hit the beige car before even realizing what was happening.

"Okay," Brandon said finally, and released the break so the car could start to crawl again. Gina knew that seemed too easy, that he let her win too quick, but things seemed to be that way with him. A shrug instead of a fist. "But you got to give people a chance, Gina," he said. "People might surprise you."

...

The first day of summer vacation, Gina worked at the Dollar General from opening to 6:00. She didn't expect to see Brandon, but there he was, standing outside, waiting for her and smiling. She knew better, but she got in his car.

"It's the first day of summer. We should do something fun," Brandon said when they were pulling out of the parking lot.

Of course, Gina knew where they were going as soon as they

turned off Greenley Road—the party that Brandon was trying to talk her into going to at Maggie Jenson's swimming pool. The pool was one of those above ground monstrosities and it sat right in the middle of a field.

"No," Gina said as Brandon pulled his car up into the grass to join the fifteen or so already there.

"Look," he said. "I've driven you around for weeks. I did that because I like you, okay? I just want for us to have some fun. Can't you do this for me?" Brandon stopped just short of saying that Gina owed him. "Besides, we're here now and I'm not leaving so you might as well get out of the car."

Brandon immediately fell in with his friends. Gina, feeling awkward and alone, stood outside of the circles, her arms crossed tightly across her chest. But then, some girls she knew from school came up and started talking to her. It got darker and she found a seat near the fire. As the flames warmed her face, Gina felt almost pleasant. "I could go to sleep," she thought.

Some of the kids were in the pool, splashing around and shouting. There was a pole light illuminating just one rippling circle of water, like a spotlight, and most of the people were staying out of the spot, in the darker edges.

"Hey." Brandon came up behind Gina and put his arms thickly around her neck. She could smell the beer. It was the first time he'd ever touched her.

"Hey," she said back. His arms didn't feel unpleasant, and she pushed down the impulse to pull away.

"Let's swim," he said, hot breath into her ear. Gina laughed.

"I don't swim," she said. "And I don't have a bathing suit anyhow."

"Who does? It don't matter. It's dark." Brandon came around in front of her and pulled her up, harder than she expected, and she stumbled into him. "Let's swim," he said again and started playfully walking her backwards toward the pool steps.

"No," she said again.

"What is with all the no's?" Brandon said. "I thought you didn't say no." Gina felt slapped. She'd known to expect it all along but was still hurt when it came.

"I want to go home."

"You can't go home," Brandon said, holding her tighter. "You haven't gone swimming yet."

That is when she started to feel panic rising in her throat. He was not letting her go, and he had looked over his shoulder, nodding to someone. Then there were other hands on her, wrapping around her shoulders, pulling up her t-shirt.

"Come on, Gina," Brandon said, moving his arms from around her to tightly hold her wrists so that she could not push him away. "You have got to lighten up."

"Yeah, lighten up!" said another boy, close in her ear.

There were three boys, maybe four, wrestling to get her clothes off. Someone pulled her shirt up and Brandon held her arms up by the wrists so that they could get it over her head.

"No! she screamed, feeling their hands on her bare stomach. She squirmed and bent inward as fingers ran over stretch marks— her baby rivers—that no one other than she had ever seen. She was powerless. She screamed louder when she felt hands tugging at her shorts, loose enough to come off without undoing the button.

"Help!" she screamed as they carried her up the steps. The boys' moods had shifted. If she'd just given in, squealed a little like a good girl and not fought so hard to be free, then they would have kept laughing and it would have been a game, but now it was war and they had to win.

At the lip of the pool, the boys did a half-hearted one, two, three swing. When she was out over the water on the last swing, they all released and she did not fly as much as flail out and down, her bare skin smacking the water. Then it was over. Gina's head broke the surface without her even trying, or she might have stayed under, stopped fighting to breathe. She was sputtering and every part of her stung.

Somehow, she had landed just in the circle of light, spotlighting her weakness.

But then she remembered that her body was also a strong one that could have a baby and then not have her baby, it was a strong enough body to get her out of this pool.

As she got to the side, Brandon reached down for her. He grabbed her arms and hauled her up easily, which made her furious. Another of the boys tried to hand her a towel, but she pushed it away. She knew they could probably see through her wet underwear, through to her flat, skinny ass, but she didn't care. She wanted out, away, gone.

Gina grabbed her clothes as fast as she could. People were giving her a wide berth, so she knew that she must look crazy, or crazed.

"Come on, Gina," she heard Brandon say behind her. "We're just having some fun."

She pulled her shorts on and turned to him. He was still up on the pool edge holding a can of beer as though nothing had ever happened. He looked at her for a minute, and then, it was as though he stopped recognizing her. He shrugged and turned his back to her. Gina was on her own, but she knew how to walk.

She had not even gotten to the first ring of cars before she heard the whistle, and then a buzz as something flew over her head. She heard more laughing, then another whistle. They weren't just shooting bottle rockets; they were shooting bottle rockets at her.

A third bottle rocket grazed her shoulder. The pain from the sear made her stop. They wanted her to run, but she was not going to run from these people.

Gina turned on her heel and stomped back towards the laughing group.

She was still holding her t-shirt in her hand and imagined now that she looked like some sort of warrior instead of a weak girl. She picked up speed as she ran up the steps. When she reached the top of the rickety wooden stairs, she did not slow, but charged at Brandon. She saw his eyes go wide and the smile fade from his perfect mouth just as she reached him and sent the palm of her hand pushing hard and fast into the base of his nose. There was a satisfying feeling of soft skin and bone giving under her hand. Brandon's arms pinwheeled once, twice, and then he disappeared backwards into the darkness of the pool.

A nose will bleed a lot, and the last thing Gina saw before she turned and started back down the stairs was red sneaking out of the dark water into the circle of light.

She'd pulled her shirt back on and she could feel the fabric sticking to the burn on her arm. That would hurt later when she had to peel it off and the burn would probably leave a scar. "Good," she thought. Maybe that's what she needed to remind her who she was, and who she could be.

No one was coming down this dark road to save her. If Gina wanted to be saved, she was going to have to save her own damned self.

Kathleen Driskell

Homegoing, West Virginia

After the quick service in the funeral home,
                    the spluttered amens, and
          folks who came up to pat
his waxy hand, and/or lay a palm upon
          his hardening
                              cheek, we followed the hearse
          onto WV-39, our purple flags fluttering
          to remind us we went together.

          The hearse slowed, turning onto
                    Panther Mountain,
          and went round and round
                    and round and round

                              toward the top
          where it eased to the side of the gravel road.
                    In a car far behind, I slid out
and was caught by
          wild raspberry bushes.

In the prickly red chair before the light
          of the popping coal fire, I kept my eyes
                    on Jesus's blue eyes
                    over the mantle, above a long gun,
          after he'd called me to sit in his lap.
It was before dawn,

                    before others,
          the women, of the cabin had awakened.

          Now, I watched some of those same women, older
                    now, around me, kin, pull off
their good church shoes, reaching
into back seats to grab sneakers or slip-ons.

My grandfather's pallbearers, his
            sons and sons-in-law, transferred
      the casket from the hearse to
            the back of a pickup truck, bulging
      wheel hubs so rusted
            they looked like lace
that might snag or tear our skirts.

Then, Uncle Skeeter slapped the truck's side like
      a horse's ass, twice hard, and the back
                  tires spun a bit in the loose gravel
before grabbing, lurching forward.

      Later, around a table filled with deviled eggs
and green beans with new potatoes,
            they admonished me for wearing
      my high heels to his grave-side—see how
                  they'd been wholly ruined
      on the mountain, sinking
                  deep into the moss and mud.
I chewed on a ham biscuit, a bit of pink gristle
            catching in my mouth. I swallowed that
                  I'd come home just to delight
      the man was dead, wishing only
            that my heels had been able
                        to punch holes
            through his putrescent
      heart while he was yet living. Putrescent, I chewed
more on that greasy word, a word
            I imagine I learned
      only by leaving.

Kathleen Driskell

Study on the Indigo Bunting

Preening in the Beech Tree
This morning, you, dazzling
in an unexpected place,
the leafy crown of a beech tree,
sun lighting your iridescent
blue-black coat shimmery
as a tuxedo jacket worn
by a boy I hardly remember.
As I walked down the buckling
driveway behind him, catching
my high heel when he opened the door
of his father's car for me, just
the way his father had reminded
him to, then helped me tuck in
the satin edge of my skirt, romantic
as the lining in a casket, I fingered
the violet orchid corsage on my wrist
and wondered how far
I might go that night.
The next dawn, it was
birdsong that bore me back up
three concrete porch steps
to my family's house.
Glittering high heels in hand,
I stopped at the door for a moment
before walking in, thinking, then,
I'd done it, and would enter
as someone new, someone not
afraid, perhaps still broken,
but now loved.

It would take years to learn
the infinite ways
there are to be broken,

but, also, the infinite ways
to heal. It would take years,
too, to learn that you,
pocket-sized blue bird
I treasured so much, are but
one half of the pair that returns
each April to find new love.
I turn from you, your cheerful
song, to search in the trees,
I'm looking for the homely female,
common-looking as a brown wren,
snug in her open-cupped nest.
She's harder to find, but that,
too, I've learned, means she's more
likely to survive until next fall,
to lift off again, to wing to
some tropical place, navigating
her way there by the stars.

Kathleen Driskell

Fairest of All

Two hours earlier we'd zipped
each other up, stuck bobby pins
in one another's hair, tucking them
into our special updos. We borrowed
pink cologne and rhinestone earrings
to wear. We'd lovingly stroked on blue
eye shadow and shared lipsticks,
caring nothing we said about catching
something from one another. And now
we stood together at the dark edges
of the gymnasium, a rented glitter ball
throwing sparks across the concrete block walls,
and we fidgeted, unaccustomed to our high heels,
seeing that the cutest boy in school, dark bangs
across one eye, was walking toward
us. We'd not even noticed that a moment before
he'd rolled an apple across the dance floor,
and it was now resting, bruised, at our feet.

Lynette Ford

Chores

Cobwebs white with dust
shroud the corners, windows, walls,
thin ghostlings gently waving,
waiting for the light to change.

She makes tea, hot water poured
over two lemon ginseng tea bags
pressed into the stoneware mug
her sister gave her long ago.

She casts a cleansing spell
over her sister's house,
stirs the brew, drinks in meditations,
pink thoughts on a gray muslin morning,

plans for corn broom and dustpan,
for rags and cedarwood polish,
for lye soap and sunlight
to wash away sighs and uneasy endings,

to clear the frail yet constant weight
of dusk-tinted memories. It's time, to clean.
The mood of seasons is changing.
A crocus blooms in slowly melting snow.

Roberta Schultz

Maurice (Song)

I find him on the dam in the morning
where he takes off without warning,
avoiding any camera angles I might try.
He sails across the lake in just two flaps—
lands up in a shagbark with few gaps,
but I still spy that long bill standing by.

Chorus
He's the center of attention, and he knows it.
I named him for a favorite poet,
but pronounce it like that famous song and dance man from France.
I try my best to capture his pizazz,
but he's not down with all that jazz.
He's got something going on at the nest
that requires his very best Maurice, um-hmmm. Maurice, uh-hmmm.
Maurice, um-hm- hm-hmm. Maurice, um, hmmm. hmmm.

He's keeping down our bluegill population
while supplying ample fascination
for this tree-huggin', nature lovin' sometime photography fan.
Though I know I'll never capture his best grooves,
I'm inspired by the grace of his nest moves—
how he gathers grass and cedar for his mate's new rookery plan.

Roberta Schultz

At Valenti's (Song)

Who is that man with the menu in hand
at Valenti's. at Valenti's?
What does he see when he walks up to me
at my table in the corner?
Years of sweet memories, our heads nod in time,
watching the dancers while sipping red wine.
Cheers for the old days when we looked as fine
as this guappo, guappo young man.

Down at Pangallo's we'd danced under lights
while the old men played at bocci.
Back in the courtyard, Peluso's upright,
slightly off-key Liberace.
It was the 50s, our town was the spot.
We had a club where Sinatra was hot.
Now I just sip my Chianti a lot, and remember, remember those nights.

Oh, out on the floor we'd glide to the other side of the ballroom.
Chandeliers glowing crystal bright. We would dance all night
like a bride and her groom.

Now, there's a bar with a restaurant attached
serving Mazzei's ravioli.
His mother's pasta, he makes it from scratch,
and that film crew sings his praises.
I ask to sit in the old room instead where
bright colored plaster cracks halo my head,
missing that old neighborhood so long dead—
all those guappo, guappo young men—
who I wish I could dance with again.

Roberta Schultz

Little Fallen Star

Little fallen star in a Mason jar.
On and off, your beacon pulsing light
throws some magic at the night.

Sprinkling fairy dust on this carbon rust,
tickling grumpy clouds to sneeze,
and now you're sailing on the breeze.

I will have to set you free.
Like this light that shines in me,
we can't stay lit inside a jar locked tight.
No, we're gonna have to lift the lid and breathe.

Little mystery, rub some glow on me.
I will never fully understand,
though I've held you in my hand.

There's a tiny speck of your angel fleck.
Like a timbrel in a Psalm,
it's dancing at the center of my palm.

I'm so glad I set you free,
'cause like this light that shines in me,
we can't stay lit inside a jar locked tight.
No, we're gonna have to lift the lid and breathe.

Little fallen star in a Mason jar.
On and off, your beacon pulsing light
throws some magic at the night.

Marjorie Maddox

Mountain Fence

Line after line after line,
what does Fence think it can contain?

Not parallel trees. Not curved mountain.
Not circumference of sky, clouds' dimensions.

Not intersection of blue/gray/black/brown. Not morning sun
rising above every calculated boundary of man.

Lisa Kwong

The Importance of Anniversaries

Lately, I've been thinking about why anniversaries are so important to me and my family. In addition to wedding and graduation anniversaries, my immigrant family celebrates the following:

-when my Dad swam from mainland China to Hong Kong
-when my Dad first arrived in the US
-when my Dad opened our family restaurant
-when my Mom and older siblings arrived in the US
-when my parents each became US citizens

2024 is a momentous anniversary year for me:

-5 years since I gained a church family and got baptized
-10 years since I received my MFA in Poetry
-25 years since I graduated high school and started college

In 1999, I was preparing to graduate high school in Radford, Virginia, while Ngin Ngin, my paternal grandmother, continued to worsen after surviving two strokes. She was bedridden, continued to lose weight, and lost control of her bodily functions. I felt afraid, not wanting to visit her. Her favorite grandchild had always been H, my younger sister; Ngin Ngin had raised her since she was a baby. In return, H never wavered in her love for Ngin Ngin. She gave Ngin Ngin her insulin shots and did not recoil when Ngin Ngin had soiled herself. In fact, I remember H glaring and chastising me for being grossed out. Through clenched teeth, she said something like, "It shouldn't matter! She's still Ngin Ngin. She still needs us."

High school graduation is a big deal for any teenager, but even more so for me and my siblings. I would be the third person in our family to graduate from high school; for family and economic reasons, my parents did not receive beyond a middle school education in Tai Shan, Canton, China. Also, I was more than ready to move on from high school. Sure, I had a few friends and my peers voted for me as the girl Most Likely to Succeed, but often I felt lonely on the bus rides to quiz bowl competitions and away football games as part of the marching band. Everyone would be chatting away, and I would be lost in a million thoughts, including family responsibilities like helping at the restaurant. I hated my body, believing I was bigger than almost every girl in my graduating class. I'd love to tell you that I was an amazing student who did no wrong, but my academic performance was plagued by procrastination, missed deadlines, and a failure to understand Honors Physics and AP Calculus. In high school, your worth as a student seemed to be measured by whether you took the most advanced classes.

So, I was very excited to graduate but understandably worried about Ngin Ngin. I prayed for Ngin Ngin to not die before I graduated. After the first stroke which took away her ability to speak, I still talked to her wide-open eyes and closed-mouth smile while she sat still on the couch with her walker and me in front of her. I remember telling her about God's salvation because I grew up in a Baptist church and had learned you needed to beg God for forgiveness and then be saved. I held her hands, and she nodded, her brain still alive in her damaged body. I kept praying Ngin Ngin would believe and go to Heaven.

Up until that point in my life, high school graduation day was the most exciting day for a teenage me. A few hours before the ceremony, I sat on the floor in my bedroom, yearbooks in my lap, not believing I had made it after all of my academic failures. Another exciting memory was that one of my poems would be read at the ceremony by my friend who was class president. Despite my mistakes, I had actually done well with poetry that year. I was co-editor of our school literary magazine, I had won two local awards for my poem "Lost Seashell", and unexpectedly, I was awarded the senior English award, an honor that I thought someone else deserved because they had taken AP English and I had not (I failed to complete the summer reading list). When it was my turn to walk across the stage, my older brother said I stepped as if I was about to meet the President of the US. Unlike Brother and Sister, though, there was no big graduation party that filled the restaurant because Ngin Ngin was close to death. We had a smaller celebration with our immediate family and employees.

Summer came and went, and soon it was time for me to begin college at Appalachian State University in Boone, North Carolina. To be honest, I don't remember how I heard of ASU. However, when I was applying to colleges, I was looking for schools with music programs and ASU had one. I actually got into their School of Music at the last minute. Without any adults at home to guide me (Brother and Sister were both living and working in other states), I didn't know that I was supposed to sign up for an audition date back in the fall or winter. I called the clarinet professor, and he agreed to let me submit a cassette tape audition even though it was already April. To my relief, I was accepted.

By the time I arrived at ASU, I had a schedule which I'd registered for during summer orientation. It included Pre-Calculus, Introduction to Music Industry, Music Theory, Freshman Seminar, Expository Writing, and Clarinet Lessons. However, I was quickly informed that as a music major, I needed a major ensemble and had to take Marching Band; I had not planned to continue after high school. I found out, though, that college marching band was much different and more fun. You got to do different shows every game and didn't have to worry about ranking high in competitions. While I was late in joining, most people welcomed me, invited me to lunch and dinner, and helped me get caught up on our first show. I even developed a crush on one of my fellow band members, and some of us went out to karaoke where I sang "Believe" by Cher. Besides an eight am Pre-Calc class, my first two weeks of college were going well.

On Friday of the second week, I decided to stop by Belk Library and check my email since back then, we still had dial-up internet in the dorms. I logged into hotmail, and this two-line message had arrived from H:

come home.
grandmother died last night.

Stunned, I immediately called home, and plans were made for one of my Dad's long-time kung fu students to drive me home to Radford for Ngin Ngin's funeral. On the way, I remember trying to process Ngin Ngin's death with Dad's student but also sharing the excitement I'd already experienced in college, including the boy I liked.

I don't remember everything my family did to prepare for the funeral, but one moment stands out. Before the viewing, Mom was fretting about what to wear, so Sister was helping her by rifling through dresses in Sister's closet. Meanwhile, not knowing any better, I kept repeating, "It doesn't matter." Sister shut me up by saying, "Lisa, this is your grandmother, not some teacher. So it does matter." I understand now why it mattered what we wore to Ngin Ngin's funeral and how I was being insensitive, but the teacher part of Sister's comment was also insensitive. Two of my science teachers died while I was in high school: Mr. S. from cancer and Miss T. from suicide, both devastating our community but the latter incomprehensible to her students who had no idea how she was mentally suffering.

This was the first time my family had buried one of our own in the US. So, you could say that some of my relatives didn't know the American norms for mourning. For example, people are supposed to wait in line to see the casket during the viewing, but my extended family—aunts, uncles, cousins—crowded all at once around Ngin Ngin's embalmed body and made-up face, sobbing and shouting their grief in Taishanese, my family's hometown dialect.

We are a Chinese American family, so we wanted to maintain Chinese mourning traditions but also follow American protocol. White is the color of mourning in China; Americans wear black. We compromised by wearing white tops and black pants or skirts. There are some customs we did that I still need to learn the significance of. Before we went to the gravesite, we tied white towels around our arms. After Ngin Ngin's coffin was lowered into the ground, we were each given small green leaves, told to air-wipe our eyes with these leaves, and then turn and walk away from her burial spot without looking back.

Twenty-five years later, I still miss Ngin Ngin and feel her presence every time I read the poems I've written about her. When I think about how far I've come in fashion (I finally embraced my body in grad school), I think of Ngin Ngin the seamstress who made matching blue and purple floral dresses and red and black paint-splattered white pajama pants for me and H. I still regret avoiding Ngin Ngin when she was dying, but I have tried to forgive myself. I am still trying.

Anniversaries are reminders of events in our lives both big and small: joyful, traumatic, and all the in-between. For me and my family, especially my parents, each anniversary reminds us of the strength, sacrifice, and courage it has taken to arrive in the present. The larger the anniversary, the more we feel our aging, but I'd also like to think it means we are still here. We have persevered, survived, and thrived. It is a privilege and honor to be able to commemorate every year living past the biggest moments of our lives.

Odana Chaney

A Flower is Just a Weed You Care to Look At

Gather the pine needles to make our bed,
Soft and secret in the scented dark
Press your hands into shapes of prayer between us,
Asking forgiveness for the things we share

Hide my body from the shame of the stars with yours
Keep me covered and just for you
Call me your soft, wild thing
Name me after the flowers that perfume the air
The moon doesn't need to know what others call us

Take from the valley what is left
Pass through the trees on your way home
And remember to face the sun-soaked dawn,
A sweetness, like morning glories

Devin Aeh Canary

the sprite and the troll

my best friend's poems are tiny manifestations of her
cute, light, and flighty
funny, often unintentionally so
short, like they can't stand to be in one place for too long

mine are like me too
heavy, dark, and mostly sad

every morning we read each other's work
i tether her down
so she doesn't float away
she lifts me up so i can feel the light

Jessica D. Thompson

Sky Daughters

We flee into a stand of trees
in search of scriptures

written upon leaves. Envying
the braided bark of hickories,

we storm rushing streams,
ghost horses with red manes.

Our moss-soft names
are lost to memory like fire-

pinks whose petals
have come undone.

With hearts billowing
like cumulus clouds—we are

the descendants

                of rain.

Amy Le Ann Richardson

Outgrowth

Tendrils of vines untamed as your hair
wrap life around these cold metal poles

we drove into the ground

racing up as fast as they drop
reaching roots through soil

explosions of limbs and soft green leaves
velvet like your skin

growing in every direction, just as you are,
lanky arms, legs, and torso

stretching for more.

April J. Asbury

Beyond the Fair, Beyond the Tender

Come down, ladies, from the smoke over the mountains,
    Your pain isn't waiting to claim you again

Come down from the pedestals, let your rubies spill;
    watch your treasures catch moonlight,
    your secrets sing in the nightbird's sob
    and the lullaby of leaves, of oceans
    you never lived to see

Come down from the obelisks that bear your husbands' names
Let your veils trail over dew-gemmed grass and cast
    away the starry crowns you earned
    at the cost of all your dreams
Dance in the creek's glass and silver braid
    and leave off the shoes that bent your feet,
    rubbed pain into warped bones

Come down, ladies, the funerals are done
    no presents to wrap, no casseroles to cook
    no sick children to tend, no pins and pennies to hoard
Come down and, if you wish, grace us
    only with yourselves
    not bound by what we needed—
Come, dance for your own sweet joy

Kristi Stephens Walker

Nesting

When your wife died, you asked me to proofread her obituary,
and I read it like a biblical scholar exegeting a sacred text.
I smiled when you wrote that she could flatfoot a hole through the floor.
After that, you began feeding mourning doves.
All that winter you listened for their call, tending them with care.
I tried to do the same for you.

Mourning doves are seasonally monogamous,
usually beginning courtship rituals in the winter,
and waiting for spring to begin work on a nest.

"Life is short and love is big," you said to me,
in the wee hours of that chilly March equinox,
under cover of moon song and ambient light.
We cooed until the sun peaked over Paris Mountain.
I did not yet know the lengths I would go to for a nest I could not feather.

Wendy McVicker

My grandmother once danced

with a troupe of Indian
dancers, stepping
easily out of her life
to become their soloist
for a week. Dark

and slender then, she
fit in well, her brown
eyes shining golden
and her sleek black hair
rippling as she moved.

I can see
the gas–lit theatre,
the heavy red curtain
rolling back, light
flickering off bracelets
and teeth as tongues
slowly hush, and then

the eerie music starts,
flute and stringed sitar
uncoiling in the high room,
twisting among the crystals
of the chandelier, and my
grandmother, Hazel, lithe
as a wand, draped
in bright silks, one
slim arm gesturing,
reaching, her form suddenly
as purposeful as an arrow
pointing toward a future
unimagined until that day.

Sarah Diamond Burroway

Summer 1977

Box elder and black cherry in the yard outside our windows,
sturdy with low, curved branches for swinging
or sitting, and dropping off on the deep ditch side,
always trying to stick the perfect landing at the street's gravel edge.
That summer, Carol and I tired of tomboy games, so we climbed the tree
to hide from the world with our new treasures:
a cast-off purse from my mom, and Avon lipstick samples—
peachy orange, fuchsia, frosted red.
We smoothed their beveled tips against our lips,
no longer having time to put up with the pests who were our brothers.
We admired our painted mouths in the smudged mirror
of an empty Revlon compact, its powder puff still beige, stale scented.
We pressed our mouths against the backs of our hands and laughed
at the shapes of our kisses and marveled at the rose-toned stains
on the ends of our twig cigarettes, snapped from the smallest branches.

Danielle Kelly Curry

Storm on the Horizon

Layla wants to look back but doesn't because contrary to what her momma told her there ain't nothing good ever worth looking back at. Lonnie's truck tires spit out dust from this godforsaken road hidden miles away from her family's property. The dirt flecks sting as they hit her, but she doesn't dare flick any of it away. She's alone now. That's all she's ever wanted.

The wind picks up and flattens her red curls against the nape of her neck. For a moment, she reaches to tuck the loose pieces behind her ears but stops because she fears Lonnie will take it as a signal and come back to get her. Just like her hair she don't know what restraint means any more.

This morning's talk with Lonnie and her mother was the last straw. She can't help but replay his smooth, drawn-out voice in her head because it is as much a part of her as the storms that used to keep the crops on the family farm growing.

They had sat around the kitchen table, the one her father made from odds and ends furniture that he wasn't ready to retire. The top dipped and cracked in places where the wood had settled over the years. Lonnie had invited himself over, like he'd done the last month and a half since her father passed. A field hand, Lonnie had worked for the family, doing odds and ends on the farm when crops came in for the last few years, but recently too many storms had flooded the crops and there was nothing left for him to take care of on the farm. Except Layla.

"I know you've been through a lot," Lonnie said, "but, I'd like to change that."

"Don't even," Layla said. She kept her eyes trained on the table so she didn't have to see him.

Her momma, Jean, brought over some coffee, and situated herself between Layla and Lonnie. Outside, the clouds gathered in clumps and slowly turned from white to grey.

"When will these storms be over?" her momma asked.

"Not soon enough," Lonnie said.

The three of them just sat there. Lonnie and Jean looked out at the storm over the horizon. Though Layla didn't like coffee, today she withstood the bitterness.

"Jean, you know you'd be better off selling the farm, now. It's too much work. The weather, with this global warming, or whatever they're calling it these days, isn't helping matters," Lonnie says.

"I know. But Tony loved this place."

"And you can still love it, but not need to run it. Give it to me."

"And why would she want to do that?" Layla said. For the first time, she looked up from her coffee and straight at Lonnie.

A smile slowly spread across his face. "Because—" Lonnie trailed off. He reached for her hand on the table. She pulled away.

Layla picked at a knot in the table plank closest to her. Ruined was the word her mother liked to use when talking about the table and the family after her father died, as if the two of them couldn't survive without a man. Ruined. The word felt like sandpaper on Layla's tongue.

"—I want to marry your daughter," Lonnie said.
Layla kicked back her chair and it hit the floor with a thud that felt like it shook the room, "What the hell?

"I don't think you heard him," her momma said. "He wants to marry you."

"I heard him, alright," Layla said, "but that don't mean I want to marry him."

"Hush-up, child." Jean leaned towards Layla, then stood, corrected the overturned chair behind her daughter, and gathered the coffee mugs to place in the kitchen sink.

Layla loved her momma, but she had this all wrong. Lonnie had tricked her momma in the same ways he had tricked Layla herself into thinking he loved her.

He had caught her eyes the first week he'd started working on the farm, and by his second week, he'd convinced Layla to meet him in the field. So, she'd brought out a blanket, smoothed it between the rows of corn they'd planted with withered stalks, and packed a sandwich for both of them so they could talk for a while because when Layla had talked to him, she felt like everything stopped in the world just so she could be heard. But as they'd sat there together amidst the crops and dirt, the wind changed. She could still feel his hands in her hair. The way when he pressed his weight against her, she fell back. Her back couldn't settle flat to the lumpy ground, so she dug her nails in the dirt surrounding them, until there wasn't any more room for the dirt to creep in.

Since then, she tried to stay away from Lonnie when he was over helping her father. She wanted to tell her momma what happened but was too late to make any difference. Layla had gone and scrubbed her fingers raw for days just to get the dirt out from under her skin. Even while in the kitchen with him, she felt like the dirt still stained her skin.

Lonnie stood and moved over to the now vacant seat beside Layla. When she backed away from him, he leaned in closer. "Honey, there ain't another one like me who will take someone as damaged as you."

If she was being honest with herself, she knew what he said was true. She knew it. Her momma, probably even knew it, which is why her momma didn't bring in the only white dress they had in the home, but instead, came back with some faded dress that Layla had never seen before.

"This will work, won't it?" her momma had said.

"Only good girls wear white." Lonnie crossed his mud-crusted boots in front of him as a slow smile spread across his face. He leaned in so Layla could hear him: "And you and I both know you never been good a day in your life." He then turned to Layla's momma holding up the best dress they owned in the house. "I sure don't care what she wears. The only thing that matters is that ring on her finger that makes her mine."

The three of them sat at the kitchen table like some messed up version of the holy trinity. Layla couldn't speak. Didn't care to. Who would listen? Layla nor her momma knew much about the inner workings of the farm. Layla knew she could figure it out if anyone would give her time to figure out her daddy's system. She could do it. She could.

They all stood up from the table. Her momma handed her the duffle bag with some clothes, including the dress.

"Time to go, so we can beat this storm." Lonnie stood and took the duffle bag from Layla's hands. "You can change when we get closer to the courthouse."

Layla stood up. "Momma, we can do this. It may take time but it's what daddy would have—"

"Your daddy would have wanted the farm in capable hands," Jean interrupted. "Go, on. Now." She placed her arm around Layla and pulled her into her chest. Layla backed away.

Capable. The word hung in the thick, sticky air as Lonnie

and her mother ushered Layla out of the house. Above the house, the clouds joined together until the sky turned a silver blue and the horizon disappeared.

…

Now, Layla plants her feet in the gravel and layers on the white dress to stay warm as the temperatures drop fast and the wind turns against her.

A black crow lands nearby, and Layla meets its eyes. For a few seconds the two look at one another as if making sure neither will interrupt the other's journey on the now empty road. The crow extends its neck, and lets out a caw before releasing Layla's gaze. The smooth black feathers turn deep blue in the waning light as Layla moves in tandem with the crow, cautious not to interrupt it once more.

The dress dances in the wind, but it's more ivory now than white as the dust settles around her. But none of that matters right now. Not one person could take the dress away from her. Not her momma. Sure as hell not Lonnie. Layla may not have been good but she damn well knew she looked as good in ivory as her momma ever did look in white.

Sharon Waters

Pondering the Blue Ridge
—with acknowledgement to Angelina Weld Grimké

Tell me is there anything lovelier,
anything more grand
than the rise of a mountainside
held to by deer, fox, and bear
for cover—for home?

Is not each rock a tale of its
rise from glacier mass?
Is not each tree a poem about the
mineral bed nourishing life?
Is not each fossil a torch song
for what was and what will be?
Is not each human footprint
an interruption?

Morgan DePue

Bloodstream

Tell me what the river
knows of stone.

Tell me how each crick
resembles bone.

Tell me how water runs as blood
in every thousand-year flood
drenching hollers ev'r' other month.

Tell me how what feeds us
also grips us by the throat
how each drop of water
bears a price of 6 pints of blood.

Tell me how there's nothing
          to be done
how there's nothing
          to be done.

Susan J. Mitchell

Beautiful Survival

The hummingbird hovers near the bushes with
the most delicious flowers. Nectar sweet as
morning fruit. Wings a blur of delicate,
musical feathers.

She glides from one bloom to another,
backward and forward, side to side. An elegant
display of daily living. Like a woman, comfortable
in her own skin, striding into a crowded room.

Miriam Nordine

writing in mud

As a kid, I got to know my environment by stripping through layers. Tearing the bark from trees, stabbing the ground with a shovel, grass, roots, worm ways unearthed.

My juvenile wishes were to bathe in clay, mix concrete, stack bricks, woman the crane. My mother more traditional: Clean the mud off your feet. Come sit and read at the table.

I learned that the best clay lives near the creek, responds like a sponge, no taming necessary–intuitive building block. Eventually, words connect like wet slip.

It's rare that pores don't clog, that tension rods don't break word associations. Takes a special person to tell a story that makes sense–resisting the wind's whims.

Pencil breaks ground, chicken scratch narrative, ideas at work wearing hard hats. Meet at the cherry picker, rising to an aerial view of the so-called site of innovation.

Bitten off more than we can stomach, but the job always gets done. The business of creative construction, ingenuity or technical skill. What do you bring to the table?

Danita Dodson

The Mother Tree and Me

When the world weighs heavily upon me,
I wrap my arms around the Mother Tree,
as I reckon the Matriarchy of Mamaw,
midwife of a life she seeks to rescue.

I wrap my arms around the Mother Tree,
communing with a strength grown before me,
midwife of a life she seeks to rescue,
identified by deep roots as her kin.

Communing with a strength grown before me,
reading the lines she has written in bark,
identified by deep roots as her kin,
I feel her rise from the ground to know me.

Reading the lines she has written in bark,
as she casts her long hill-woman's shadow,
I feel her rise from the ground to know me,
seedling child that I am competing for light.

As she casts her long hill-woman's shadow,
her limbs reach down to regenerate me,
seedling child that I am competing for light,
holding me midair 'til my own space opens.

Her limbs reach down to regenerate me,
as I reckon the Matriarchy of Mamaw,
holding me midair 'til my own space opens,
when the world weighs heavily upon me.

Danita Dodson

Truthteller

It was you who first storied me dark truths.
No other adult dared past Dick and Jane,
but you sang for me grim mountain ballads
and told the tale of a cold-blooded killing
you'd witnessed in a churchyard in your youth,
a child's hard memory shared with a child.

You didn't need to tell of grace, light, and
the unfolding beauty of holy love
because you were all those good, perfect things.
I knew them seeing you move midst flowers,
and I knew them when you presented me
gingerbread communion in rose-scented hands.

Since the other wicked things were harder
to see, you taught them to me through bold tales.
Perched on a black vinyl couch with my feet
dangling, I tilted my face toward yours,
fixed in a lockjaw pose as I heard tell
of the Booger Man who hounded bad folks.

I almost swear you hoisted a painting
in front of me—very tenebrific—
watching me as I gasped and flinched to see
that woodland haint with fiery eyes and horns,
but when I asked you years later, you said
that you'd only described one you once saw.

Mamaw, my hill-woman scop, you shaped me
to shun the very appearance of evil,
so that when I fled your dark-word portraits,
slamming shut the screen door to seek sunshine,
I saw God move midst flowers, presenting
gingerbread communion in rose-scented hands.

Sarah Pross

Butterweed
—after Wendell Berry

The pasture, bleached and cold two weeks ago, now erupts
in a fury of yellow-topped flowers. A pony wades
through them, knee high, munching as it walks.
We are driving, speeding past field after field
when she asks what those flowers are.
I don't know if it's right but the only answer
I find online is butterweed and I fall in love
with the sound of the word, roll it around
in my mind for days. They could be
any number of things—marsh marigold,
canola, scotch broom—but I like butterweed the best.

Laura Grace Weldon

Bio: 100 Words Or Less

Deep under this street
are footsteps of those
who walked here long before
land was bought and sold.

Inside the aroma of cut grass
wait old growth ghosts—
oak, hickory, sycamore.

Behind a child's nightmare
of wide-mouthed predators
lies her ancestors' vigilance.

Curled in my arm's memory
is a doll I carried through a
tippy toe world of talking flowers,
singing bees, steps leading
to an underworld lit by lanterns
all the way down.

Kristine Williams

Before Dawn, Gura Road

In the single digits, it is mind-numbingly cold,
not that my mind has caught up to my body,
which dressed in the dark, by touch and the memory
of where I threw clothes on the floor by the bed,
before I got between chilled, white cotton only a few hours ago.
My shirt is on backward I realize,
tag scratching the hollow that sucks in when I breathe,
although I am trying to take shallow breaths
through the collar of my puffy coat
so the hair inside my nose doesn't freeze.
I am ankle-deep in snow
while my dog picks her way through the yard
trying to find the perfect place to pee
and I am trying not to be irritated
because I was, after all, the one who gave in, got up,
snapped on the harness and leash
(coyote yip-yips earlier have made me cautious).

But now that we're here,
I see how the snow glitters where my flashlight touches,
flakes dance, caught in the beam,
and above, the Milky Way, gauzy,
and suddenly I remember a box of letters I found once:
two women writing to each other through winter and a pandemic,
their words reaching out, connecting,
were a life raft, driftwood from a sinking ship,
something to cling to in the middle of the vast, deep blue
and, buoyed by the memory,
I stop and the universe unfurls above.
Snow hides the ugliness of winter, crunches beneath my boots,
and I stop my breath,
listen to the blood whooshing in my ears,
a train whistle, the dogs down the street barking,
anticipate the warmth of the bed,
knowing you will roll close no matter how cold my skin,
hold me until I can sleep.

Megan Krupa

An Ending

Look at the way time stops// the way it doesn't// the way every mother/ holds another/ in her heart/ Like the Mother / who lost a child/ for the world// because his death meant salvation// Whom did she turn to in her grief?/ I need to know/ how she kept living//because all mothers/ lose their children/ in the end/

Cathy Cultice Lentes

What To Believe

I stroll the river path in Pomeroy, Ohio, on a Sunday morning. I walk here often, the Ohio River to my right on my way out and to my left on my way back. The path is quiet on Sunday mornings, and I am often the only one on it at this time. Sometimes, I just walk, watching turkey vultures circle above me, listening to Canada Geese squawk low across the water. I smile as fat groundhogs waddle off the path and dive into one of their ever-widening tunnels. I step over dog poop and avoid discarded fast food wrappers. Today, I'm listening to a podcast, a weekly teaching by Buddhist Tara Brach. She is earnest and funny and true.

...

When I moved to southeast Ohio in 1987, I was a young mother of a toddler son and pregnant with my first daughter. I had come here under false pretenses, though I didn't know that then. I followed the man I was married to, the man I still believed in, the man I had pledged my faith to, though he had tried hard already to break that faith and trust. I kept finding reasons to believe, to negate my worries and forgive his anger and narcissism. I was determined to live up to what I had promised, to make a go of this family, to discount my doubts, to never go home to my parents dressed in defeat.

When we arrived in Pomeroy, there was no river path, only a disused railroad line, and the river with a broken bridge, one I prayed over any time we had to drive it. The simple ferry that carried us across the current for a time to West Virginia was a relief and balm. I trusted the old rough barge more than rusting steel and cast pillars. Either way, I guessed, I could die, but that ferry gave me a feeling of security. People had long believed in boats, had perfected this mode of crossing. Besides it was closer to the earth, and I was a child of dirt and trees, a lover of mud and bark. I was taught to believe in my creation.

...

As I walk back to my car on this Sunday, church bells ring out calling folks on both sides of the river to gather. Ohioans and West Virginians alike. The old bridge is long gone, replaced by a wide modern span. The ferry no longer needed. The toddler son should be a grown man, and was briefly, spectacularly, before being ripped away from us in a freak accident. The baby girl I carried is grown as is her then undreamed-of little sister. The husband gone along with his broken promises and lies, like that old bridge, no longer feasible. Though I firmly believe in love, I am unsure if I still believe in marriage. I am alone with my thoughts and uncertainties. I have not set foot inside a church in years. What do I still believe in? What is left of my faith?

...

When I was a child, God was a given presence in our lives and there was no question of going somewhere other than church on Sunday mornings. I studied him as he lived in a book of Bible stories, well-illustrated with color panels meant to draw the young eye in and keep it there. Old Testament stories did this best, full of magic and battles, giants and heroes, many-colored robes. I sensed him in the soaring arches of the Springfield Central Methodist Church, the great noise of the pipe organ, in the calm safety of Sunday School. Though once I devolved into sobs when I forgot my offering money. Would God kick me out? I was unsure of the rules and he was almighty. Early on I took to heart the message that I was sinful and must be saved. I tried and tried and tried to be a good girl, always feeling I fell short in the eyes of my parents, and therefore God.

My parents and grandparents believed. I tried to please them, to find the peace and security they appeared to find in their ideas of God, but the line between learning and sin seemed fuzzy. Though an only child, I never seemed to get it right. When they watched the Billy Graham crusades on TV, I watched too. Stadiums full of people listened to Graham's silky voice rise and fall, preach and call, and when he asked them to accept Jesus Christ as their savior, thousands answered, coming down and down from the far reaches of the cheap seats. "We'll wait," he crooned each time, and he did, as music played, and my parents from their very cheap seats in the TV room echoed, "Amen."

The pageantry and rituals amazed whether in the great gathering of people at Central Methodist, the intimacy of my grandparents' one-room country church twelve miles down the road, or the prime-time traveling colossal of TV preachers. Each time the call went out, I expected that this time the wave of Jesus would catch me, and I would ride high on the water of passion, speak in tongues, feel deep inside the fire of righteousness that could not be doused. Each time afterwards, I still felt myself, small, disappointing, less than, as if my prayers weren't earnest enough, as if a door had been closed in my face, and then the lock clicked shut. I felt most alive, most found, most seen, singing rhyming choruses of hymns, hearing the lilting music of King James liturgy, walking in green cathedrals of forest, and feeling the secret power of words rising within me.

The evening before Grandpa Cultice died, my parents and I had done the usual Sunday rounds. Church, dinner, then off to visit their parents, and if I was lucky, my cousins, too, would be there. First, we drove to my mother's parents who lived in an old farmhouse with a ticking mantel clock, clear plastic protecting the sofa, and depending on the season, muskrat pelts spread on the cellar door, or bluegill and sunfish glinting in a bucket near the outdoor pump ready to be cleaned and descaled. After a couple hours in Selma, Ohio, we'd drive back toward Pitchin, turn left on Jackson Road winding toward the flat acreage of my Dad's parents. Having come from tenant farmers, there was no ancestral land, only a long list of rented properties, and this modern one story in a line of other simple homes. The atmosphere on Jackson Road could be tense. That night though, Grandpa cooked, and wanted us to stay for supper. We did. I remember laughter, and a bear hug as we said goodbyes. It was the only time I remember him hugging me. And though I noted it, I was worried about getting home in time to watch The Wonderful World of Disney.

The next morning, I woke to the sound of Grandma's voice in our kitchen and crying. What had happened? I lay in bed afraid. After a while, Dad came to my door, tears in his voice, tears in his eyes. He moved my desk chair to sit beside my bed.

"Jesus came to get Grandpa last night," he said.

An image of Jesus sneaking through a window like a thief came to me clearly as if he had come in search of money or jewelry and taken Grandpa instead, and then a sinking feeling of guilt swept through me because I had hurried us home after dinner.

...

The summer after Grandpa Cultice died, we headed west on some sort of National Lampoon Vacation though that had not yet been invented. Interstate 70 was finally complete, wide open to travel, and there were relatives to visit in Arizona and California. Dad piled the car trunk full of suitcases, mother packed the snacks, and I was secured between my maternal grandparents, Pap and Grams, on the back-bench seat straddling the floor hump with my feet, swaying north or south as exits for rest areas and Stuckey's presented themselves.

Though I'd always been drawn to the lyrical language and ascendant music of church, it was from that back-seat perch heading west that I found my soul. The world was a wonder, and I took it all in, state by glorious state bringing daily miracles.: from the glassy-eyed trout served to Grams for supper one night and her own wide-eyed reaction, to the citrus trees laden with lemons and oranges on a strangely green school lawn in the Arizona desert. Terror filled me as a dust storm shook my great-aunt-and-uncle's trailer outside of Phoenix like a small tin toy, and then washed it, and dried it fast as an automatic car wash when a towering thunderstorm roared through, wind and rain and hot air blasting.

Those evenings in Arizona, a neighbor girl, Cathy with a K., and I shared dreams, fortune tellers as only ten-year-old girls can be. We sat across from each other on the scratchy grass, knees touching, as dusk enveloped, and a rainbow dimmed. The sunset lit distant mountains in pinks, purples, and orangey reds. I've forgotten her hopes, her deepest desires. But mine: a writer, I said. I'm going to be a writer. And we both believed.

...

When Grams died of a heart attack at age 84, I was bereft. I had two little ones at home, and a husband rarely home. The news sent me sprawling to my church along the river where I found some small comfort in the home and arms of the preacher and his wife. But at the funeral in Gram's ancestral Indiana, I couldn't staunch my tears. I sobbed for losing her, but for other losses too. Without her, my childhood was gone. I could not say all that I felt. How alone. How lost. How none of the promises made to me felt kept. How the life I had envisioned had not come.

When my third child was born, one I willed into being knowing even then I would need her, I left the church after long struggles with faith using this third child as my public excuse. My chapel became the wild woods around me. My true center, the words inside that filled me. My own promise, the one I followed.

...

In 2021, my mom and son both gone, my dad moved to assisted living, I dove into cleaning out my childhood home, into the unknown and known of my creation. My parents married eight years before my birth. Articles clipped from newspapers and magazines led me to believe I was longed for, but hard to conceive. My mother, unprepared for the brutality of birth, said no more children. And there weren't. She died that way as well, two short months after my son, her will gone to endure any more. But my sleuthing also turned up evidence of a woman who longed for a creative life, as her mother did before her. Women who believed that some lack in them, some harbored sin inside, accounted for their joint failures, weakening bones, and unbearable arthritic pain. Did they hope so strongly for the promises of heaven because domestic life on earth failed them?

Dad kept faith, I think, until the end. His Bible, always close. He financially supported his church, even when he could no longer physically attend. Some remembered to support him. As he weakened in 2022, still recovering from Covid-19, newly sick with Influenza, one of his best nurses held the phone so he could talk to me.

"I don't know what to do," he cried.

"You don't have to do anything, Daddy," I reassured, trying to stay strong, keep tears away. "It's time for us to take care of you."

And we did

...

I walk the river path. It's Sunday morning. Church bells ring out around me. Each step brings me closer to something. What to believe?

I believe I was loved, am loved. Imperfectly. As I also love.

Faith is a path with many turnings, and dead ends.

I have seen God in a geyser at Yellowstone and the fire-filled sky after a Montana storm.

I have worshipped among giant redwoods and prayed at ocean's edge.

God waddles like a groundhog, and lifts like a great blue heron from the gravely creek bed.

Sin is a dodge, snake oil in an amber bottle.

We are born good.

We have nothing to prove. We have everything to prove.

I believe in my own creation: honest dirt under my nails, each daily journey blessed and sacred, my hard-earned cheap seat in the crowd of life.

Someone (God?) gave me a gift of words. I use it.

Sara Pisak

Patch Town Daze

—Dedicated to my great-grandmother, Nana Tina

The soil loves us and loves us not.
We are flowers yanked from their native fields and repotted.
With hands stiff and tired, I sit under fresh stars and new stripes,
sowing stitches green to white, white to red,
our heritage-striped seams of the flagpole torn from
each other like petals plucked from flowers by the spring winds.

We are tomatoes uprooted from the vines,
twisting and weaving their timelines across the garden,
dropping their fruit into the sauce I stir upon the stove.
Below the soil, their sprouted roots of latitude and longitude,
try to grow deep enough to lasso you from the anthracite cave,
before the hard coal hardens your lungs.

Before chiseled fissures in coal, invade your lung's crevices and I
rush the kids from the last church pew to your bedside,
stamping footprints in damp soil every Sunday single file
down the road like ducklings following their mother, as quickly
as you followed canaries to choke on fresh air.
Before your last exhale burns out and we never reap what we sowed.

Violet Rae Webster

So Much (Song)

I miss the music; I miss the song.
I miss the places where I belong.
Long for your laughter, imagine your touch.
Time only shows me I miss you so much.

Cry every day now, choke back the tears.
Expressing feelings, revealing my fears.
It's not a weakness to long for your touch.
It's only human I miss you so much.

Years have passed now, and it feels like yesterday.
I thought at last, how these grey clouds would drift away.
But the memories are strong and still linger in the air
Around me, everywhere.

You are my person. I am your mage
Conjuring stories up here on this stage.
Sharing emotion—exceedingly rough.
No way to anchor. I miss you so much.

I hear the music, I feel the song,
I see the places now where I belong.
And there's that laughter that goes with your touch.
Time only shows me, I miss you so much.
It's only human that I miss you so much.
No way to anchor 'cause I miss you so much.

Violet Rae Webster

You Make Me Whole (Song)

A vision of life that could be.
A someone who stands next to me.
Not facing the world on my own,
Forging a pathway.

Who knows where decisions can lead.
Lifted up or left to bleed.
Finding that partner and friend,
Committing a lifetime—to the end.

You are my everything.
You make my heartstrings sing.
You're deep in my soul.
You make me whole.

The gift of together is rare.
Another with passions to share.
Weathering all ports in the storm,
Creating a future.

A love that can stand test of time.
It seemed that at last this was mine.
But love plays a trick on the heart,
Reaching a crossroads—then apart.

You were my everything.
You made my heartstrings sing.
You're still deep in my soul.
You made me whole.

A vision of life that could be.
A someone who stands next to me.
Now facing the world on my own.
Forging a pathway—all alone.

Jessica Cory

Power Dynamic, May 2023

Hours ago, Oklo Inc. shared
plans for Piketon, Ohio, to grow
both of its next-generation
clean power nuclear fission plants.
The return of jobs for its two
thousand residents, the paper's

digital print implies. The siting papers
are filed & soon Oklo's shares
priced at ten cents apiece will be two
dollars or more. Stocks growing
pockets fatter as the field's plants
are stripped for this next generation.

The parents of this generation
filed affidavits, talked to local papers,
exposed how the A-plant's
practices endangered their lives. They shared
their cancer screening results, growths
invading thyroid glands, rates nearly two

times the national average. Two
miles from the old site, a generation
went to middle school, their growing
bodies subjected to U-235, the newspapers
report. But word of mouth shared
their stories decades before, tales implanted

like misplaced cells, explanted
by doctors, who divide tissue into two
sections for biopsy. The bad news shared
over & over with each new generation.

We carry our diagnoses on folded papers;
their scientific terms don't excise the growths

spreading in our organs. Yet growth
is always promoted. We want our plants—
knee-high corn, emerald soybean, paper
mills—to be better, stronger, available for two
or three or more future generations
so they might have prosperity to share.

Kudzu is an invasive growth on Ohio farmland. Two
hundred years ago, plants were sold to a generation
who believed its papery leaves and sweet blossoms worth sharing.

Judith Sornberger

Still in It

After thirty years of trying to convince my Women's Studies students to call themselves women—not girls—I've recently appeared in my small-town theater's production of Calendar Girls at age 66. Those familiar with the play, or the 2003 film, remember it as the one in which midlife—and older—Yorkshire women pose semi-nude for a calendar to raise money for their village's cancer center. Our theater board in conservative Tioga County, Pennsylvania, hotly debated whether to do the show. Wasn't it a bit, well, unseemly? Even dirty? And where would they find six women far past their supposed prime in our rural area willing to take off their clothes in front of folks they'd no doubt run into at the grocery store or—God forbid—church. There had even been rumors that, if we put on the play, there might be protestors outside the theater.

In real life I've played the roles of professor, mother, poet, and hard-charging feminist—a woman (not a girl, thank you very much) who prided herself on being as liberated as they come. When a friend involved in local theater encouraged me to audition for the play, I was both flattered and terrified. I read the script and found it hysterically funny. Why hadn't anybody ever mentioned that aspect? I loved the scene when Chris, the ringleader of the group, appears at a Victorian Christmas fete sponsored by the Women's Institute, the stodgy ladies' organization the "girls" belong to, in a sexy little Santa suit, scandalizing their uptight leader. Her friend Annie asks if that's not the outfit she wore to their millennium party years earlier. Chris nods and replies, "And I'm still in it, babe. I am still in it." Despite my being farther than ever from fitting into the slim, lineless feminine ideal, my much younger friend seemed to believe I was "still in it"—still bold enough, self-accepting enough, and, perhaps, even hot enough to go for it. But I'd never acted before. Even more concerning than revealing my heavily flawed body to hundreds of people each night was the possibility I'd reveal my lack of acting ability and my atrophying brain. After an academic career and enough publications to call myself a writer without risking embarrassment, why would I want to try something new that I could fail miserably at? Half the time I couldn't even remember the names of colleagues I'd taught with for years when I met them on the street, which didn't exactly bode well for memorizing lines. Perhaps it was the need to face down those fears— something I'd always been good at, however much I quaked in my boots— that made me decide to audition.

Walking into the theater lobby where the auditions were being held, I immediately discerned that I was the oldest—by at least fifteen years—and the fattest of the other women present. And I know damn well that I'm not the only woman who immediately looks around at nearly every gathering to assess her clothing size and age relative to the other women around her. By the time several more, younger, thinner women walked in the door, greeting each other—obvious veterans of past plays—it was all I could do not to hoist my plus-sized ass out of the wooden folding chair that had given a tell-tale squeal when I sat down and skedaddle out of there. But having my friend Lilace, who was also auditioning, sitting beside me kept me seated. As I waited to begin, I squirmed in my chair, trying to get comfortable. My short legs, with their full thighs, weren't crossing these days unless I used a hand to pull one over the other. Instead, I crossed my ankles to one side, a "ladylike" pose I was taught in 7th grade Home Ec (all I remember except how to make scrambled eggs), wishing I'd returned to Weight Watchers months ago.

I've always been told I have a nice voice, so at least I had that going for me. As a seasoned teacher, and a poet who'd given many readings over the decades, I was used to performing. And, at 66, I wasn't as self-conscious as I would have been at 26. Furthermore, when I really thought about it, I didn't give a damn anymore what anyone thought of me—one of the truly liberating aspects of advanced age. The atmosphere was pretty low-key as the director, a guy I'd known slightly from around town, asked us to take turns reading different parts. I did my best at a Yorkshire accent, gleaned from many years watching Masterpiece Theater, and tried to use inflections and voice changes to interpret each of the characters I read based on their lines and what they were doing in the scenes. After an hour, the director thanked us and said he'd be in touch. I left feeling I'd done my best and proud of myself for trying something new.

And I did get a part. The part of the oldest of the calendar girls—fifteen years older than her cohorts (typecasting), a retired schoolteacher (also typecasting, I supposed). But only seven women had auditioned for those parts, so being one of six chosen wasn't much of a distinction. Nevertheless, I was thrilled. My character, Jessie, had a caustic wit that I adored, maybe even enough to learn her lines. At our first rehearsal, as we waited for the director to begin, we burst into a discussion of which body parts we were willing and not willing to show in the scene in which the "girls" are being photographed for the calendar. Even the slimmest among us were quite particular about which parts they felt comfortable revealing. One had small breasts she was ashamed of. Another didn't want to show her drooping belly.

I recalled the time I showed my students a video of Lucille Clifton reading her "body part" poems. As the goddess-sized Clifton read "Homage to My Hips," in which she refers to hers as "mighty hips" that don't "fit into little, petty places," hips that "go where they want to go" and "do what they want to do," I'd watched delight breaking over the young women's faces and heard a few giggles. They were amazed by the way Clifton had taken a culturally-defined negative and reversed it into a symbol of power as the poem ends: "I've known them to put a spell on a man/and spin him like a top." I asked the students to make a list of three of their own body parts they loved and another list of three they hated. The hate list had been easy. They hated their butts (too big), their noses (too big), their thighs (too big). The love list took longer. I saw writing and scratching out. I heard sighs. Although they were reluctant to admit loving any body parts, a few said they liked their eyes or their feet, their hair or their hands—parts that are rarely culturally judged as good or bad. One older student said she loved her arms because they could comfort her children. A member of the women's cross-country team loved her calves because of their strength. So they also could love body parts for their functions. Not one mentioned loving a body part that gave her pleasure.

So which parts did I still love? And which were I willing to expose to an audience? I'd liked my breasts ever since they'd sprouted when I was twelve, or at least once I stopped being embarrassed by the nipples poking through my blouses before I got my first bra. In my first two-piece swimsuit at fourteen, I finally caught the eye of the cute lifeguard at the neighborhood pool. And a few years later, I liked them even better the first time my boyfriend slipped his hand inside my bra to stroke them. Who'd have guessed that touching that part of the body would electrify everything else? Even now that my breasts are mostly fatty tissue and quite droopy, I'm still quite fond of them. When my fiancé, who I'd met at age sixty, called them "world class breasts," I assumed he was referring to their DD size (definitely the breasts of a woman, not a girl), but he said that, while he found their size delightful, he especially liked the pale rose color and suckable shape of the nipples, and he loved how responsive they were. Woo-hoo!

My character Jessie must have been okay with her breasts, too, because her only stipulation when she agreed to pose for the calendar was "no front bottoms!" I was with her there, but I would have said—and did—that I would show no bottoms at all. I'd once been proud of my round and firm backside, but its roundness had gotten way out of hand, according to my own standards, which, of course, are not really my own but are gleaned from every swimsuit page in ever catalogue I allow through my front door. Not to mention all the years I'd been schooled by fashion magazines and visions of svelte young actresses on TV and in movies.

My legs were okay from the knees down, as long as you didn't look too closely. The calves were muscular and tapered down to shapely ankles, but the blue veins bulging like a spider nebula on the outside of my left calf were unsightly as hell. Practicing Tai Chi for the last six years had strengthened my arms, but you'd never know it to see my flabby upper arms or the crepey skin hanging beneath them. Later, in a scene where we all were supposed to don glamorous black dresses, I would be the only one wearing a floor-length gown with sleeves.

The more I thought about it, the more I wondered what the hell I'd been thinking when I signed on for this show. In Scene 6, during which each of our characters would pose for her calendar shot, Calendar Girl Celia suddenly has second thoughts just as the camera is about to snap her photo. Annie, another Calendar Girl, reassures her, saying, "Look, none of us are used to standing in front of people naked, love. Even husbands." Karl and I have been together four years, and I still prefer that he doesn't see me completely nude. He, on the other hand, paraded around in his birthday suit the morning after our first overnight. Of course, he hadn't received daily messages since the day he was born that just about every one of his body parts (at least the ones that showed) was flawed and needed fixing, a message that grows louder and more insistent as women age.

So the breasts it was. Jessie is a knitter, so during "her" turn, I held a basket of yarn balls to cover all but my voluptuous cleavage and wore a knitted shawl draped around my waist. The other "girls" were showing a lot more skin, their props covering less, but we agreed on a no-nipple policy so as not to scandalize our neighbors and bring down fire and brimstone on the community theater.

One night we spent four hours rehearsing that one ten-minute scene over and over, trying to get the timing and blocking right, trying to get our bathrobes off and on again quickly without leaving too much exposed. Afterwards, I overheard a couple of the other Calendar Girls talking and my name mentioned. Later, one of them told me they were talking about how brave I was. I was immediately offended, assuming they meant I was brave to show off my overweight, old body. But before I had a chance to get huffy, she said, "We are so impressed that this is your first show and you're doing THIS show." Oh. All right. I guess I was pretty amazing, at that.

When we'd first started dress rehearsals, we'd all been as modest as my seventh-grade friends and I had been in the locker room trying to get in and out of our gym suits without anyone seeing us in our underwear. But gradually, we became more and more comfortable with each other, and with ourselves. One night I told "Celia" that she had such pert nipples, I couldn't believe she'd breastfed her babies. Another night, one of the skinnier "girls" remarked, in a voice tinged with awe, "Jessie [my character's name], what beautiful breasts you have." Backstage, there was just a half-drawn curtain between us and the male lighting technician, as well as the male actors (who did very little clothes changing, while we changed for nearly every scene). By opening night none of us really cared if that curtain was open or shut. Between scenes clothes flew in all directions as we rushed to get back on stage in time for our cues. Even I had lost all self-consciousness.

When we'd finally gotten the getting-nude scene in shape, our male director remarked, delighted, that it had the feel of "a girl's night out." It's true that, among the characters, there was lots of laughter and dancing around as we downed shot after shot of pretend-vodka to prepare for our photo session and hooted and cheered as each of us was photographed. But it was hard work disguised as fun. The real fun was hearing the audience's laughter throughout the show, especially the women's laughter—raucous, conspiratorial, as though they were up there with us, behaving with outrageous abandon. Behaving like a bunch of girls who'd never felt shame—who'd never yet had periods or breasts to harness into bras, who'd not yet donned the heavy mantle of womanhood. One weeknight, in between performance weekends, three of us went to see a move that some would call a "chick flick"—*The Book Club*—featuring an ensemble cast, like ours, except these actresses were famous. When we walked in just before the lights went down, the only seats left were in the front row. "Are those the Calendar Girls?" a woman shouted from the back of the theater. We stood, turned, and waved. "You ladies have great big balls!" she yelled. The rest of the audience, many of whom told us on the way out that they'd seen the show, roared and applauded. Although "balls" were body parts none of us had ever claimed or longed for (whatever Freud said), we appreciated the compliment. Call us what you liked, we were "still in it"—still pushing the boundaries of acceptable female behavior, trying new and scary things, claiming our sexiness despite age or body type, and, perhaps best of all, empowering other women to do the same.

Tracy Staley

Cheap Thrills

At the Marathon
on the Mountain Parkway,
I wait for my mother and grandmother
to slip inside the bathroom stalls

before I begin my examination of the
narrow vending machine
mounted to the concrete wall:

The Original French Tickler
Stimulates ecstasy

and then, the photo:
a spiky
pink-tipped tube

50 cents,
various colors!

A second photo:
a woman,
mouth open,
head thrown back,

blonde hair fanned
like feathers.

Back in the car
my mother remembers,
a time from life before me:

a trip to the beach
a coin-operated motel bed—
25 cents to make it shake.

Ali O'Rourke

Mother's Boyfriend, or Door Number Three

He would recreate gold nuggets by melting down jewelry
from pawn shops and retirement homes
then drizzling the molten metal into a bucket of hose-cold water,
aiming always for the upturned sweep-end of the broom;
the splash sizzled and steamed,
a trinity of matter taking form.

Just east of his single-wide trailer, where roaches
shared the couch with me,
his mid-July workshop hunched chill and dim,
smelling dank, like our fifth-grade field trip to the Mark Twain Cave
when the tour guide turned out the lights
to show us what true darkness meant,
somehow reminding me of the taste of blood in my mouth.

Selling those "24 carat" chunks to fools at the fairs—
Barry Apple Festival, Tom Sawyer Days—
he and I conformed to an unspoken bargain:
I held my tongue to his chumps; he never touched me.
They believed they were getting *The Real Thing*—
a genuine gold nugget mined out west, put to sale
next to rows of knock-off Bowie knives, seventy-five-cent sunglasses,
Snap-N-Pop fireworks for the kids.

How could they be so gullible? These grown-ups
buying the shiny lie from a sunburned, sleeveless, stain-shirt man
in a black cowboy hat at a sweaty street fair?
Even at eleven, I knew
the rare water gun I was afforded
wouldn't last the day—
wasn't quality,
the barkers' giant prizes were poorly made,
and the grab bags for a dollar would never open
to the treasure
I was hoping for.

Ali O'Rourke

Dandelion Shades
—with apologies to Yeats

I can't bear those ghosts
on my neighbor's front lawn.
My own yard sleeps dreamless,
abandoned of ethereal wonders.

In daylight, those buttery chums
purred the bright birthright
of interlopers everywhere.

But motionless now in dim streetlamp-glow,
they whisper of loneliness,
all suburbia-colored.
I almost forget what they used to be
and only see
their vestiges—
hollowed orbs,
odes to emptiness,
a gazeless crystal ball,
heartless star.

This fearful, fragile existence—
clinging to their second coming,
soon those tender centers will not hold;
one easy breeze and they
drift away—
bodiless night-floating shards of
Used-To-Be
light.

They make me tiptoe.
I hold my breath to write.

Ali O'Rourke

For Papa

I am clay shaped by time spent in your hands.
Childhood, after all, is a choiceless path.
You erased my Self like a message in the sand.

Forcing fingerprints and alms into my hand,
You beggared me—a subtracting sort of math;
I was shaped by too many years spent in your hands.

You burned all maps; escapeless- no lands
Were safe, nor landings—left in hurricane's path;
You erased my life like messages in sand.

You built bonfires of my dreams—hope was banned.
Division of family—a hateful form of math.
I was diminished by years spent in your hands.

My half-formed body could never escape your hands
Until I dug you out of me—a jagged, fleshy swath—
I released my Self; your hands grasp only sand.

You thought to hold me, but freely now I stand;
Reborn from blood and water, a baptism more than death.
Re-formed to rise again from the fire of your hands,
I washed you from my life, like tracks from sand.

Nicole Karch

Those Summer Saturdays
–for Ginny

When Uncle Frank hurled fistfuls of rock to draw out the water snakes,
you popped a hand over your plucky ways and waited.

Even you, a wild chicory stalk of a girl, knew he was
the closest thing Chandlersville had to a saint.

The strip mine pond churned. Transverse waves, explosion
of reptile, all those slick shocked bodies ribboning

away from the rocks and onto the far shore. You and your cousins
admired the frantic snakes, their scattered and water-whipped

dance for survival. Though back then you didn't know it was
survival. You didn't see the brokenness lying latent

in your cousins, who would someday blaze unruly like ditch lilies.
What you saw was Uncle Frank, all muscle from the rough business of farming,

how he patrolled the pond edge and examined his handiwork,
how he rarely proclaimed love but in one booming order: "Go!"

And you felt his love in the steady gaze he held over the water
as twelve boys and girls launched themselves into it.

The pond shattered and righted itself around your body,
buoyed you up like an offering to the sky. The boys tried

to shove you under, but you slipped away from them:
kicked off, dove yourself down, down, down

to the diaphragm of what industry left behind,
your heartbeat and muffled laughter humming in your ears.

It sounded like a hymn.

Chrissie Anderson Peters

Don't Ever Stop Dancing

Megan Morgan stood in the bridal dressing room of the Main Street United Methodist Church in Langston, a small town in deep southwestern Virginia. Her mother and bridesmaids fluttered about her, all in a tizzy about her big day. Her cousin Ruth Ann, her maid of honor, seemed to be the only one who saw through the makeup-and-mascara façade. Her eyes met Ruth Ann's, a family renegade who had refused to get married, even when she gave birth to her son Andrew, bucking local tradition and small-town doctrines in doing so. She admired Ruth Ann, respected her for doing things her own way. Ruth Ann wouldn't be caught dead walking down the aisle to a man who had molded her to be what he wanted her to be, to a man she wasn't certain she loved. Ruth Ann would never give up her own identity as Megan had during the three years she and Paul Mullins had been together.

It had started out so romantically. Someone of Paul's stature and importance in a town like Langston paying any attention to a wanna-be country singer like Megan, much less a Morgan, a family not even near the social ladder, was a wonder. But as time wore on, Paul told her that a woman in his social circles wouldn't run around singing country music, playing music in bars in Carters Corner with her high school friends. It was time for Megan to grow up and put those silly notions behind her. "Besides," he told her more than once, "country music is so undignified."

Megan said her contact lens had gotten stuck on the pretense of going across the hall to the bathroom at the church. In truth, she was about to start crying and didn't want to burst out in front of her attendants. She grabbed her makeup bag and cell phone, assuring them she needed no assistance. Her long, white silk gown, as elegant as it was, had no long train for her to trip on. It was just eight feet across the hall. She would be back in a jiffy.

The bathroom was packed. She opened the door and immediately closed it. She ducked into the custodian's closet, out of sight. For a moment, she couldn't catch her breath. She couldn't remember ever being so uncomfortable. She thought of her maid of honor and two bridesmaids in their lovely lilac dresses down the hall. She needed to figure things out. Fast. She didn't relish the thoughts of just running away, but she also couldn't envision marrying the man waiting for her at the altar. Paul had his good qualities. But theirs was not a match made in heaven. She had sacrificed so much of who she was for so long, she wasn't even sure who Megan Morgan was, anymore. She knew full-well who Morgan Mullins was supposed to be, though. A high society lady, a pillar of the community. A lover and patron of the fine arts. Which didn't include country music.

Megan exhaled and fidgeted in the darkness until she found the light switch and illuminated the little closet filled with janitorial supplies and other necessities for the church. A mop and bucket, broom, and vacuum cleaner piled against the far side of the closet. Lined up on the shelves, she saw rags and various cleaning supplies. She wished there was a chair. Maybe sitting down would put her more at ease. She needed to think. So she leaned against the janitor's sink and drew in her breath.

The door flew open, and an old woman stepped inside, closing the door behind her. She looked startled to see Megan. "What in the world are you doing in here, child?" her voice shook as she closed the lid on a toolbox, making a seat for herself, making a crowded space even more crowded.

"I'm thinking," Megan stammered. "What are you doing in here, Miss Alma?"

Alma Mullins pulled a flask from her shiny black pocketbook, which perfectly matched her shoes, and answered, "You're thinking—and I'm drinking. Here's to us!" And she took a long gulp as she toasted the young bride-to-be.

Megan watched in awe as Miss Alma, the matriarch of one of Langston's finest families, chugged from the flask. Miss Alma, who had celebrated her ninetieth birthday here at the church just last month. It was surreal. Miss Alma shook her head. "I know you've seen people drink before, so close your mouth before something flies in there, child!" She paused, then reached the flask out to Megan. "Forgive me for not offering sooner, would you like a drink? It's been a hell of a day. I didn't want to come today, nothing personal against you or your fiancé, you understand. I'm just an old woman, and I get tired of making the social circuit simply for the sake of being paraded around town because of who I am and the fact I'm older than dirt."

Megan politely declined the bottle. Miss Alma shrugged her shoulders and took another swig. "Weddings always get me worked up," Miss Alma explained. "Ever since my own. Now that was a hell of a day." She closed the lid of the other toolbox and put out some rags on it from the shelf. "Since you're here and they can't start without you, you might as well pull up a seat and get comfortable."

Megan wiped the toolbox down and looked for the cleanest rags she could find before sitting down. Even though she wasn't sure she wanted to walk down the aisle, she also didn't want to ruin the gorgeous gown her parents had spent good money on. "Why was your wedding day so awful, Miss Alma?"

"Well, for starters," the old woman began, "I was in the family way and upchucked every ten minutes. You young people weren't the first to do the horizontal hula. It happened back then, too. And back then was 1950. I was barely 16 years old. Arnold was almost 25 when we married. And I was not what his family was looking for in a daughter-in-law, I can assure you!"

Megan's eyes widened more with each detail of Miss Alma's story. "Such an age difference, you were just a girl," Megan reached for Miss Alma's flask and took a sip of vodka and passed the flask back to Miss Alma.

"You'll never look at me the same way again, will you, child? Everyone thinks I'm so stiff and well-bred. That's Arnold's family, not mine. I was a Morgan, too, like you. I was wild when I was young. Thus, all that upchucking on my wedding day. Arnold came from a 'good' family. They didn't want their name sullied. When he told them I was pregnant, they practically ushered us down the aisle themselves. But it had to be a big to-do because they were the Mullinses, and everyone expected a show. Arnold fought in the War, you know, came home a hero here in Langston, him and several other of our boys. My older sister Virginia helped out with the USO efforts up in Carters Corner. She knew all the dances and taught them to me. By 1950, I was a dancing fool. I was still doing the boogie-woogie, the foxtrot, the jitterbug… I couldn't get enough of any of it." She took another draw off the flask. "Do you like to dance, child?"

"I've never been much of a dancer, but I love music, especially country music, but Paul says it's undignified," Megan answered. "I used to sing in a little band back in high school, and we'd play at birthday parties and once we even played at a club up in Carters Corner. We thought we were big time, then," Megan giggled.

Miss Alma shook her head at Megan. "Let me tell you something, child, don't ever stop dancing."

Megan cocked her head at the old woman. "I don't dance. I sing."

"Same difference in this case. Listen here." Miss Alma put a hand on Megan's knee and repeated, "Don't ever stop dancing. No matter what happens, no matter who says to, don't ever stop dancing. Arnold didn't like that I wanted to go dancing with my friends after we got married and put his foot down right away. Said I was his wife now and a Mullins woman wouldn't behave that way."

Megan shook her head. "Must be something about Mullins men, them wanting their women to act a certain way."

Miss Alma continued, "It's because of how important they take that family name and what they think it means around here. They're no better than us Morgan girls, child. Just richer and more politically aligned. Now, listen, don't let anyone tell you what your heart finds pleasure in is unimportant, Mullins or not."

She took a tissue from her purse and wiped her lips, smudging her lipstick the tiniest bit and Megan reached over to help her touch it up. Miss Alma went on, "Don't ever let your head overrule your heart. You'll never find peace in those actions. You'll try to find acceptance for the rest of your life, but you'll only find contempt because you let yourself be talked out of that one thing you truly loved doing. And here's something else—don't ever believe that another person can provide your happiness. You find happiness on your own."

Megan contemplated those words deeply. For three years, wasn't that what she had been doing? Letting someone else think he could provide her happiness and neglecting to do that on her own? She took out her cell phone and started taking notes. Miss Alma nodded her approval. "Don't build up all your dreams on something that isn't true. If your heart isn't in it, then it's not what you're meant to do. If someone promises to love you forever but puts conditions on it, then walk away—walk away fast, while you still can. Are you getting all this?"

Megan nodded. "Miss Alma, it's like you knew I needed to hear all this. Like you knew I was in here needing to hear exactly what you're telling me. I've been so torn and confused about what to do, whether to go through with this wedding. My heart just isn't in it, anymore. It's like—I'm tired of playing a game I used to think was fun."

Miss Alma nodded, put her flask back in her purse, and smoothed her dress down over her knees. "Believe me, child, if you stop dancing, you'll look your whole life for something to take its place. And you'll wake up one day and be ninety years old and realize what you have missed. And you'll take a deep breath, child, and know that you messed up in that one moment when you looked that person in the eye and said, 'I do,' when you knew you really didn't. You couldn't because your needs and wants were not the same."

Megan's eyes filled with tears as she leaned over to hug Miss Alma. The old woman whispered, "I see it in you, child, a need, a love, a yearning so big." She stood to her feet and looked Megan in the eye as she opened the door to leave. "I mean it, child. Don't ever stop dancing."

Megan stood in the empty silence of the closet, looking down at her cell phone. So many people were sitting out there waiting for her. Paul was waiting for her, but for the version of Megan Morgan he had cultivated her to be, not the version of herself she needed to be. She pushed the door open and almost immediately met her mother's eyes, Ruth Ann standing beside her. "Megan, what on earth are you doing in the custodian's closet?" her mother demanded. Ruth Ann's gaze told her she sympathized.

"I needed time to think," she told her mother. "It's time for me to dance, Mama." And with that, she pushed past her father, who was standing at the back of the sanctuary, waiting to take her down the aisle. She burst through the back of the church like a woman on a mission, sidling down the aisle as well as she could in that long satin dress, not like a demure bride waiting to be led to her mate. Paul looked bewildered at first, then embarrassed, then angry when she wouldn't stop making a spectacle of herself as he motioned for her to stop the nonsense and do what was expected. She did stop eventually, short of where she would have met him at the altar.

A hush fell over the entire congregation. Everyone knew something was coming. And no one wanted to miss it. This would be a day that would go down in Langston history. It had that feel about it. The pastor cleared his throat and asked if they were ready to commence, hoping to get things back on track. "No, sir," Megan answered respectfully. She turned to face the congregation behind her. "I hope that you'll all find it in your hearts to forgive me for having you get all dressed up and coming out today, for holding you up when you might have had other things to do. I hope my mama and daddy will forgive me for all the trouble and expense today has meant for them. Paul, I hope you'll find it in your heart to realize I'm not who you thought I was, and it just couldn't have ever worked out. And to everyone else, especially Miss Alma, I just hope you dance."

With that, she started back up the aisle, a little two-step struggling to get out and stretch. Megan marched out of the sanctuary, relieved with her decision, amidst the whispers and shock. Her cousin Ruth Ann smiled and hugged her as she handed Megan's purse and keys to her as she passed by the dressing room on her way out of the church.

Megan went out into the crowded parking lot and slowed as she approached her own car. There stood Miss Alma, shiny black pocketbook in hand, a big smile plastered on her face. "Let's boogie, child," Miss Alma said, toasting Megan once again with her flask held high.

Karen Whittington Nelson

A Trifling

Would I cherish life less,
had I not inhaled the scent of earth and decay
before lying down in a meadow
upon a carpet of violets, lulled to sleep
by the hum of bees and busy things—

And but for the weight of the full moon,
an owl's shadow brushed my shoulder
and a vixen both acknowledged
and dismissed me
with a flick of red flame.

Mary Lucille DeBerry

A Peek at Progressive Parenting

*—A 1939 Woman's Home Companion cover featured a stylish mother
with a darling toddler with a harness on. –Slate Parenting Newsletter*

On a trip to Florida,
February, 1941,
my mother grasped tightly
my long leather leash,
especially when the organ grinder
released his monkey Bolonio
dressed in navy, red and gold,
wearing a bell boy's cap,
to roam the crowd,
to search for pennies,
to reach into my pocket.

The tan brown of my baby-harness,
for me, meant exploring out-of-doors
or digging in sand near an ocean
or riding on a noisy streetcar
where the conductor
gave me chewing gum.

Back home in West Virginia,
my mother used the harness only once:
when she was canning peaches
and I was howling, banging
against the side Dutch door,
wanting outside freedom.
This time my mother fastened
the leash securely to a redbud tree,

Old Mr. Swadley, though, hobbled by,
saw me, happy in sunshine,
stripped down to my diaper.

My mother, in the kitchen,
with the upper part of the Dutch door
open, heard him grieve.
"What kind of woman would
do this to you—would put you on a leash!"

As soon as Mr. Swadley moved onward,
she maneuvered me back inside.
I wailed at my uprooting.
My baby-harness, though, was banished.
Forever. Now, it languishes in a drawer.

Beth Copeland

You Hand Me a Heart-Shaped Stone

from the river   and I think of
how your love washes   over me like water.
How last week you said, *Breathe,* when I thought I'd lost
my wallet at the gas station. *Turn around, go back,* and there
it was!—on the ground next to the gas pump, with my license,
credit cards, and cash. How you helped me look for my dog on
the coldest night of the year, and held me as we prayed he'd be
found and he was!—that quirky old coonhound. How your love
soothes me all the way down to my bones, how the stone is
dimpled at the top with cleavage between the heart's two
curves, how solid and smooth it feels in my hand, how
when I close my eyes I can feel the vibrations of
water and the warmth of your hand in mine,
how I am the stone and you are the river,
the giver. How you said, *I will
love you always,* and
I said, *for-
ever.*

Beth Copeland

The Weight of Ashes

From a blue velvet bag, I remove the rosewood box
hand-carved with plum blossoms and branches,

a brass plaque laser-etched with his name—Phoenix—
glued to the smooth surface of the wood.

The weight of his ashes is heavier than expected,
like snow that softly falls, blanketing the mountain's

spiraling roads, heavy enough to break an old
barn's rotting beams and the limbs of brittle trees.

Mitzi Dorton

Potato Poultice

Three years old and Mama is beside me watching for my eyes to shut. The wild plum trees in the distance blur the streetlight beyond the backyard, the open window ushering in the familiar perfumes, the purple flower clusters, and yellow golden fairy hats with strings, which we pull and sip.

My father flicks the light switch separating us from the outside world.

"A splinter in your foot?" he asks.

He holds up a potato slice he sets against my sole, then Mama wraps it tight with a strip of cloth and pulls a sock over it. Their voices intertwine, like vines that mesh.

"Where'd you ever hear of that?" she asks.

"Listening to the old-timers," he replies.

I start to shift and rouse. Daddy shuts the light off again,

"Listen! Listen!" he says in loud whispers. He says it's a whippoorwill.

Then he whistles his own version,

"Whip-poor-will, whip-poor-will!"

He can make me believe anything.

I fall into slumber as it pierces the sweet and sour, roosting on a prickly fruit tree pecking on a plum. I will go out tomorrow and find the prodded plum, search for the bird in the flickering leafy shadows.

...

The next morning, my parents hover over me again, pulling off the sock, pressing my foot.

"That drew it out a little," Mama says as she hands him the tweezers.

I draw back my chubby foot.

"She's not having that!" Mama responds.

Daddy pulls over the big glass ashtray, where I tossed orange peels yesterday, dug away in bits by tiny hands, along with the smushed Lucky Strikes and peanut shells.

Look what I pulled out of your foot! he exclaims. He holds up an orange peel in the tweezers. Then, a peanut shell, "Even an orange seed in your foot!"

A cigarette butt? What! In my foot?

"It's gone. It worked," they sigh.

I breathe in the wafting summer magic, which Mama deems lilac and honeysuckle at their finest.

I am healed.

Jennifer Schomburg Kanke

Making Do

We begged Granny for Taco Bell
which seemed to us a simple request.
Even our parents, as skint as they were,
bought it for us.

It was a summer sometime in the 80s
and we were staying with her
in a mill town without a mill,
not one still open at least,
with pill mills unthought of,
still fifteen years down the road.

*Well now, I don't know
what that is.* We were horrified,
in the same way we'd been
when she told us the hill next door
where we played freeze tag and dodge ball
had been the county dump
when our father was young,
that the barbecue out back
had been made with bricks
he'd hauled from it one by one
all by himself
with his little red wagon.

She looked up Taco Bell in the Yellow Pages,
even though she'd have to ask
one of my aunts to drive us there.
Nothing was listed. At least
that's what she told us. Scioto County
didn't always have the things
bigger cities had, like how

when my father had his first
breakdown, she'd eventually
taken him to a hospital in Huntington
after trying to fix him herself.
When he had his second
and third, there was no money
for that sort of thing, so they made do
with something more local
where they gave him shock treatments
and Thorazine until he pretended
to be well, just to get
the hell out of there.

I try not to think
too much about how
his life would have been different
in a big city with a big wallet
because different isn't always better.
But it isn't always worse either.

Like when Granny put
taco shells? on her grocery list
and that weekend we talked her through
how to make tacos because it
wasn't just Taco Bell
she'd never heard of.
It all came out okay,
a spice was missing,
but we were just kids
and not quite sure
what it was or what
to do about it.

Jennifer Schomburg Kanke

Labor Day Raft Race, 1985

The boys are on the river, I am on
the shore. They cut fine figures on homemade rafts:
old lawn chairs roped to innertubes, rough logs
done up like Huckleberry Finn, and, yes,
a floating shower stall that's rigged to pull
Scioto River water, muddy and full
of dreams, from below to rain down on their heads.
My cousins—oh, they can feel it—this is their year!
The fog is thick with summer's end and cups
of percolated coffee, so they don't see
the rich kids, or rich by their standards, putting in
two kayaks, price tags still on them, held with jute
and Superglue to form a single craft.
The whole way down they'll think there's still a chance.

Dreama Wyant Frisk

Before We Left the Land

Tired of begging to go down the road to Milly's, Emogene sat on the large swing under the silver maple. She'd tried pouting for the longest time when she found out June had left her behind, but no one paid her any mind—busy eating, and forever drinking coffee and crying. Trucks had gone back over the mountain, and the pulling and shoving of the casket from the hearse to the porch and through the parlor door had taken such a long time, but it was over. Bonnie shut herself up in her room. Her grandma mostly stayed in bed, and Sistie waited on everyone. Her mom and dad had come during the night and slept in June's room. Now her dad didn't feel good.

Boring. Her good white sandals dug into the dirt while she eased the swing back and forth. She wore a store-bought sundress—flowers and pink stripes—with the wide straps over her shoulders. Her sleepy mother had told her to find it in her suitcase this morning. Then she smiled and winked at her before she fell back to sleep. The dress was a size bigger than her last one. Maybe she'd gained enough weight to stop taking the medicine.

Long ago, when they'd chained the old, battered porch swing onto the huge limb of the tree, Carl said it wasn't for swinging, but for sitting—like the glider on the porch. The swing always came into her daydreams. As if they were her paper dolls, she set different people in the swing at different times, her favorite being her grandma shelling peas or stringing beans.

Queenie lying in the grass. Now, all at once, everything had changed. She was in the swing by herself, and June had disappeared again, this time with Erron. Told her maybe Grandpa would play checkers with her.

The red August sun burned down on brilliant orange marigolds along the stone pathway up to the kitchen porch. Like a cradle, the to and fro of the large swing lulled her for a good long while from the agitation of the morning. Except for the squeaking of the porch chains, the yard was quiet, until a burst of nervous laughter from the kitchen startled her. Her mother's laugh—not a happy sound—rose above the others. She bolted to her feet. All she could think to do, and she wanted to do something, was find out what those two guys from the Air Corps were doing in the parlor. Stomping—just to hear it—she stopped on each tread before moving to the next.

A fairyland of flowers spread out in the parlor. In place of the furniture, large baskets of flowers and bright-green lacy ferns crowded the walls. A beautiful vase of red roses sat on the mantel. An Air Corpsman stood on either side of the ivory, silk-skirted platform where the coffin rested. The two men reminded her of toy soldiers, except these guys never moved and kept their gaze straight ahead, even as she saw the sweat running down their necks and into their uniform collars. Behind the casket, branches of the cherry tree brushed against the screens of two opened windows.

At first, she kept an eye on the Corpsmen, but forgot them when their stillness became part of the spell. Inside the room, the coffin looked different from when the men had slid it from the hearse. She had never seen one. An open lid showed a tufted satin lining. She circled the room once to get an idea of all the magic, then started over again and studied the baskets of flowers, especially the frames holding sprays of tall blooms. Amazing. She touched the gilded edges of a dark-blue ribbon and tried to read the card, but the writing was too bunched.

At the foot of the coffin, where the flag was tucked into folds at the corner, she trailed her fingers over the red stripes. When she stepped to the edge of the casket's opening, she pushed up on her toes, gripping the side. Her hand was close to a beautiful silk pillow with edging of lace. Then the smell hit her—like the ether when she'd had her tonsils out. As she pushed from the casket to get away, her gaze fell on a white, waxen face, and she turned and ran from the parlor—this time leaping over the steps.

She landed hard in the swing and it lurched sideways, almost hitting the tree before straightening out. When she pushed with her feet, the swing wobbled; she used her weight to create momentum, moving faster and higher. She extended her arms to hold onto the chains at each side, even though it hurt her hands, and began pumping—stretching her legs out straight. The face on the pillow? The swing strained to go higher, until it reached its peak, held still for a lofty moment, then lost its balance and careened from side to side. It hit the silver maple once, but Emogene rode it out, using her body as ballast until it returned to its normal sway. Was that the dead body? But where was Carl?

Again she pumped, but wasn't able to stabilize the movement this time. Where was June? When the swing reached its limit, it fell backward and dumped her. Like a cat, she landed on her feet with her knees bent. Nobody had seen her, except a mockingbird on the nearby fencepost. He cocked his head toward her, calling in a quarrelsome tone. She stood and angled her head back at him, and they stared at each other for a long moment. Rather than return to the swing, she chewed her nails until she thought of playing checkers with Grandpa and hurried to the dining room to find the checkerboard.

When she got to the long dining-room table, she sucked in her breath. Instead of the usual salt and pepper shakers and a round dish of butter on a tablecloth, it dazzled with cakes, pies, cookies, and breads. People had been bringing food all morning. Cakes with chocolate, caramel, and white icings filled the table. In the heat of the day, some of the icings had begun weeping, the swirls collecting little damp tears.

The flourishes in the coconut icing looked like ruffles, and before she knew it, she was running her nail-bitten fingertip along the edge of the plate where the icing puddled. She sucked it and the sweetness sent her to gathering up another, and another, until she'd moved higher up the side of the cake. All at once, gouges sent crumbling yellow pieces falling. Before anyone could wander from the kitchen and see the mess, she stuffed some in her mouth and turned the plate around to the back. She licked at the leftover smudges on her fingers, then rushed to pull the checkers and board from the cupboard.

She was surprised to find Grandpa in the parlor—he hadn't been there earlier—slumped on the settee, his glasses slipped forward on his nose. His vest was buttoned tight over a long-sleeved white shirt. At breakfast, when Sistie had told him not to wear it, he said he'd lived through too many cold winters to mind the dog days of August. His coffee sat on the table, nestled beside a tall spray of white flowers.

"Grandpa?" Clutching the checkerboard to her chest, she stood in front of him. "Grandpa? Don't you want to play checkers? Let's go out on the porch and play checkers." She kept her back turned to the casket to keep away the hospital smell.

Raising his head slowly as could be, Grandpa adjusted his glasses and widened his eyes. "Child, be quiet." He frowned and his eyes narrowed. "What's that all over your mouth?" With some effort, he pulled his handkerchief from his back pocket and pressed hard against her lips. Then he folded it and wiped the corners of her mouth. "What in tarnation is that?"

"Coconut. Pieces of coconut. It's from the cake. There's all kinds of cakes in the dining room."

His watch ticked in his vest pocket as he inspected her face.

"Let's you and me go out on the porch and play checkers." She chewed on the edges of the checkerboard.

"Stop chewing on that board."

Knowing he seldom stayed mad at her, she kept her eyes on him and lowered the board.

"Don't you know Carl is lying dead right there behind you? He's come home to be buried and live with our Lord forever."

"No, it's not Carl." She heard her voice and it scared her, giving lip to Grandpa.

"You stop that back-talking." He didn't look too mad. "It is so Carl.

He's dead and been fixed up by an undertaker for his funeral tomorrow. A lot of people will be coming here today to view his body."

"I already looked. It's not Carl." She wrinkled her nose. "And it smells awful."

"Look at you." He frowned. "Go get Sistie to comb your hair. It's all tangled up. And wash your face too."

"Don't you want to go out on the porch and play checkers? Please, Grandpa."

He paid no mind. There wasn't any use in begging him—he never ever changed his mind. When she looked through his dirty, round-rimmed glasses, she wondered how he could see. She dropped down on the settee, wishing he put sugar in his coffee so she could sneak a drink. She looked from him to the coffin, and back again. It always turned out he was right. Maybe she should try another look. Letting out a big sigh, she walked the few steps to look at the body again.

The afternoon sun streamed through the windows behind the coffin. Holding tight to the checkerboard, she stretched up on her tiptoes and swiveled her eyes so she could only see the white silk pillow. Then she straightened and took a fuller look, seeing the hair, dull and dark against it. It did look like Carl's, so she continued until she took in the strange face, shaded by the coffin lid, but as the smell of ether hit her, she backed off until her heels struck the legs of the chair.

If Carl could just be real, they could go in the dining room and get a big slice of cake, with thick, coconut icing, just for her and for him. He would wink, and they'd tiptoe to the front porch and eat the cake, and he would blow on his sweet coffee and hold the cup out to her for a sip—that's what he always did. Then they would play checkers, and she might win, because sometimes she did.

Grandpa knew all about being dead. Maybe he could die—wear his suit and tie in a casket, and put his bald head on a pillow with lace instead of sitting there and slurping his coffee. She tucked the checkers and board under the chair.

More people came—*Don't he look natural? Hard to believe he's gone and him so young. In the prime of his life. What will Helen do without him? We are so sorry. How's Bonnie? Heard she's taking it hard. Nobody should have to go through this. Was it just last summer, Carl and Emogene drove up and down the road?*

They looked down at her. One said he was Grandma's brother. She tried to remember him, but couldn't. The seats in the parlor filled, and the porch hummed with voices and the clinking of glasses and scraping of forks on plates.

The sun had moved away from the windows when June and Sistie entered the parlor, leading her grandma to the coffin. Sistie's skirt brushed against her leg. Grandma, her hair perfectly combed and braided, leaned upon them; her feet, in dark, felt slippers, dragged, and she swayed at times, once almost toppling forward. Emogene wanted to run away, but couldn't think where.

The three moved toward the casket while the room of seated friends and family turned silent and watched Grandma's first viewing of the body. When they stopped at the coffin, she looked down at the strange face for only a second before she twisted her arm loose from June and leaned over, reaching toward Carl's face. The Air Corpsman at the head of the casket rushed forward, as if to grab her hands, but Sistie stood tight against her mother, and June was in the way of both of them. A toy soldier again, the other Corpsman looked on. Her grandma pressed against the silken pillow, pushing it away from Carl's head.

A god-awful groan, seeming to last forever, came from her grandma. "That…that's not his head. What is it? What is that?"

Emogene had never heard that voice. Was it her grandma's? Something inside said, "See, it's not Carl."

"What have they done?" Grandma crumpled to the floor and her dress pushed above her knees, showing her white cotton slip.

Out on the porch, someone laughed. "Have you ever tasted a pie crust this good? It must be Mrs. Davis'. Do try it."

The hot August day continued to burn outside while in the parlor, the air grew thick. Emogene watched tears run down Grandpa's cheeks and drip from his chin. Part of her went far away.

Catherine Carter

The Haunting

It all happened here.
Maybe they should've stayed
where there was sun morning
and noon, where the scarred stairs smelled
so warmly of dog, but that place was small;
this one was new, its stairs varnished
slick and clear. Here the dogs
had to be put down: first the blind
pug, then the tall mutt. Then
things got worse. A spouse
on the couch sent the spouse
at the other end messages brimming
with acid. At the Superbowl
party, the onion dip tasted of tears.
There were the secret cell
phone, the hidden credit card,
the frozen accounts, the plague
of lies. The AC grew colder,
then glacial. Kids slipped on the steps;
the floors, tasting blood, grew sharp.
Paintings tipped on the walls,
edging toward doors
which kept whispering shut.
A stove handle pulled half away
and stayed there hanging.
The washer clawed holes in a blouse.
Though no necks broke
on the stairs, it was enough,
the house now wakened by pain
into its own nightmare life.

The great oak began bleeding
black, leaning out of the ground,
and as it fell the dirt shuddered
and groaned. Lost in the altered
dimensions, the twisting
halls which led to unsuspected cells
where no rooms had been, those within
looked at one another and spoke
the words there was no unsaying,
from which there was no way home.

Catherine Carter

Four Goldenrods

All through the drought, these four
goldenrod stalks were dauntless,
lifting aloft their feathery gold
and amber scepters, inclining their heads
like monarchs when the summer
wind stirred their harsh leaves. No thirst
could make them droop or despair:
noblesse oblige, they seemed
to whisper. *We must be strong*
for the piped rhododendron leaves'
dry leather, for the noons
when even the beautyberries droop.
But now in the first great rain
of autumn, now they can surrender,
now they lean toward the soaked earth
and brush their faces against it,
they bend their strong spines in arches
fit for cathedrals, bow
their heads, lay down their crowns.
After such need, there is no joy
like leaning to receive, accepting grace
with grace, with the whole
body, the whole life, offering up
all their pride and strength.
They kneel all day in their beatitude;
they weep clear tears of relief,
and in the field beyond,
all the star-white and iolite-blue
asters do the same, shaping springy stems
into long curves and clouds of thanks-
giving, like the faithful at their truest
prayers, where no longing
could touch them like gratitude.

Catherine Carter

Earthflash

> *—By the end of this century, what have been once-in-20-year
> extreme heat days (one-day events) are projected to occur every
> two or three years over most of the nation.* –Global Climate Change:
> Vital Signs of the Planet

Some night when this shriveling flesh's cup
of sudden fire splashes itself too high,
I'll thrash off the smothering choke of down,
pincer-plucked from some long-slaughtered goose,
and, half-sleepwalking, pad into the black
and white where the yard spreads beneath the moon
to press myself to cool and gritty dirt,
splay out in an X to return this witch-
burning volcanic sear to the restless
flow of magma heaving far below.
Then will I feel the suffocating scald
dissipate into grainy-cold white sand,
black humus, rust-stained clay? or will a mist
of warmth flush back, from an earth itself
a witch feeling the terror rise like heat
from the licking, whispering wood that's heaped
at her bound feet, earth itself a woman
in the net of her own sweat, running out
into her bitter black expanse to arch
against the void in futile pangs to ease
what's cooking her alive? over, over,
pressing her round back and her round belly
to the cold, a woman pelt-plagued by scourge
of fleas or ticks who never cease biting
and sucking, injecting her with buboes
and Lyme and with the smoky red-brown haze
of hot flashes in which she rolls and rolls
and rolls, while here upon her skin, we burn.

Rita Sims Quillen

What Horses Say

What's to be made of the field of buttercups,
a saffron sea at the bend of the road,
with the three horses
    one black with white mane and tail
    one coppered like a new penny
    one white as an angel
a triumvirate of muscled peace and perfection.

What's to be made
of thinking of 3 recently dead friends
every single time I drive past
the most laughably maudlin reach for meaning
when the real story is simple:
Time is real—
the realest unseen thing
undocumented, untouchable
a mystery deeper
than the eyes of horses.

What's to be made
of Clinch Mountain in bright spring light
butter bright as the horse's field for miles,
but just beside the gold section,
the ridge shrouds in clouds
as dark as my heart,
as if there had never been sun.
I'm tired of these poems—
just suitcases of dark
traveling nowhere.
I don't want to carry them anymore.

What's to be made
of these lines on a page
when I could just look in the eyes of horses,
lock their steady gaze like no other.
It is the deepest of dark loves,
fierce and fearless love of a father
who tells you all truths:
Don't you know?
Life is an apprenticeship to grief.
While you live your dreams
building the house of your life,
you collect all the tinder
to burn it down,
turn it into a rubble you will eventually
have to crawl out of.

So they whispered as I lost sight of them in the turning:

>   *You, the buttercups, the mountains,*
>   *horses and love itself will pass*
>   *but that deep gaze and golden light*
>   *will return, beaming out*
>   *from some other bright page.*

Rita Sims Quillen

The Mad Farmer's Wife Deals with Dolly

It was a big day:
a trip to Woolworth's with a calf check and shopping list.
She eyed beautiful coffee cups, a rose sweater.
He wanted heavier socks and a set of wrenches.

But she found him cradling a Dolly Parton album in his hands
"Slow Dancing With the Moon"
his two wide thumbs on either side
of her perfect face in the perfect pose on the cover,
a little smile on his lips she'd seen before.

The Mad Farmer's Wife caught her reflection in a mirror:
dowdy dress, greying hair in a tight bun,
sensible shoes with sturdy laces.
She put the rose sweater back on the rack.
A week later, she got a friend to sneak her back to Woolworth's,
bought cranberry red lipstick, a black marker, a silky robe
and a pushup bra like Dolly wore in the cover.

It was all worth it on Christmas Eve
when he came in from chores
found her there under the tree in the bra and robe,
fake mole under her nose, cherry lips, and a blonde wig
borrowed from her cousin, her guitar across her bare legs.
The album he admired was under the tree
with a bow red as her lips.
"My lips of many colors that the Woolworth gave to me!"
She sang and his mouth flew open,
stayed that way while she laughed,

slapped her leg, then he laughed, too, and came to her,
took her face in his hands, a big warm thumb on each cheek,
kissed her long and deep, then longer and deeper.

"You beat all," he said and reached for her hand.
"You are a mystery I'll never finish—
but come with me,
I'd like to read a few more pages."
He held her hand all the way to the bedroom door.

Rita Sims Quillen

Stains

I.
Purple is the color   of birthmarks and sunsets
of distant stars exploding   of bruises and death.
Time leaves a mark.   Otherwise,
how would we know it passed?   How could we go on,
all of it coming to nothing   just   gray hair and black dreams.
Every season contains purple   so it must be important.

II.
Today: a huge tree
bent a few feet from the ground   spine curved like an old woman's back
branches splayed   toward a small stream of sun
a hole in the dense canopy   where a spot of blue
breaks through.   It's easy to say
"Ah, bloom where you're planted.   Find the light, be the light."
and call it a day.   The shade there
is a deep pool of wine   and I float through it,
toward a surface   where light reclaims its gold.

III.
Years on, I stumble   still on the path.
My blanket of brambles   and briars no longer warm,
the smoothness of creek stones and silky dark soil
forgotten by knotty fingers   marked by amethyst vein maps
of all the dead ends   wrong turns   roadblocks.

All this is to say
it's fair to wonder   what purpose bad luck serves.
May we receive grace—
an orchid or mulberry or magenta grace—
for questioning why   we sometimes root
where conditions require   a crippling
to survive.

Jennifer Browne

Buried Stories, the Beloved Dead

Every Sunday morning after mass, I'd stand before the rack of prayer cards, tiny printed paintings of the holy family, the saints. I'd scan to find St. Lucy, virgin martyr, holding out her gazing, bloodless eyes on a plate. She plucked them out, or they were plucked. The story shifts depending on who's telling it, but the consistent bit is that her eyes were—that she was—too beautiful to survive intact. God fixed new eyes into her sockets, but it was the pair on the plate that followed me, at which I stared.

I learned from the holy martyrs that bodies become partial, wounded, sacrificial. Christ holds his burning, lance-pierced heart out as a child might hold a rock found on a walk, expectant of your taking it in wonder.

And in my mother's family, amputations, lost parts of selves. My Great Uncle Bob was timbering when he lost his leg, his bakelite prosthesis an unstrappable magic trick. His brother lost an eye in an accident no one can remember. Gaps darken mouths. My uncle joined the priesthood, became a genealogist marking himself a stubbed branch in the family tree, the rear-pointing triangle of *no children*. I think of women who left, who made the choice to stay, the ways in which they carved out portions of themselves to make space. And deaths, whole bodies become lost limbs.

My Great Aunt Olive was only six when she died of croup, 1901. Five years later, my grandmother was born. Throughout her life, she placed flowers on the grave of the elder sister whom she never knew. She taught us all—her children, her grandchildren—to note the location of the plot, to visit.

There is no stone on which to place a bloom, but I think about the miscarried child for whom I was an understudy. Not what they might have been, but what they might have meant to my two-years-younger parents. My mother spoke of that pregnancy when I was near to losing my own, and after the ultrasound swept and caught the electric pulse of a fetal heartbeat in my blood-slicked body, we did not speak of it again.

So many buried stories, unmarked graves across which I step and feel a shiver. No one in the family spoke of Ray, my great uncle, who left home for California and never returned. He had two marriages, and I see his second wife on his arm, pinup-slinking Mulholland Drive, but the only facts I know are birth and death dates, names, the number of his plot in the same cemetery as Elizabeth Taylor.

I imagine lives for him, ordinariness and joy, wrongs suffered and enacted. And I imagine him greying, making the trip to buy his plot, driving the funereal avenues of Forest Lawn, touring the marked graves of stars fallen in Hollywood. Bogart and Errol Flynn, Carole Lombard. Tom Mix. Maybe he had seen Mix in *Catch My Smoke* in a theatre in Cumberland in '22: the pretty girls, the men back from the war.

In this cemetery, streets named for trees. Olive Ln. An ache, there, in his memory, his long-dead sister, the other side of the country. Did he feel the pull back into the Mid-Atlantic when he made the choice to buy Lot 1445, Space 3? And what of Mary Mack, buried one year before him in Space 4? Was she anyone to him?

Is he, for that matter, anyone to me? Less real than his elder brother, Vernon, whom I also never knew, but know through his unsigned brushstrokes on the murals in City Hall, know through an obituary naming him a veteran of WWI, know through a photograph, a story of his "spooky, melancholic temperament," his greeting a person by lifting his hand to his heart.

And though I don't know what it meant to him, I love this gesture, feel it moved by his seeing one whom he loved, who could have been anyone.

This signal to the heart: my grandmother at mass, touching her chest with her hand at the time of the Confiteor, though that moment was lost in 1960's *Code of Rubrics*. Through eighty years of Sundays she made this gesture, and though I hadn't been taught that acknowledgement-made-prayer, I felt from the fullness of her eyes that I was already supposed to know it.

I stopped visiting the family cemetery, but developed a habit of touching my sternum when passing places connected to my beloved dead. It was a way to keep my grief within me, to press it back down.

A memory: a professor stands before a class, demonstrating an apology for some hypothetical wrong. He holds out his fist as he says *Mea culpa*. He beats his breast. He again says *Mea culpa*, beats his breast. *Mea maxima culpa*. A third strike.

My grandmother did not give her grief: her brothers lost or wounded by labor, by trauma, by service. Her first son dead in childhood from osteomalitis, his body left in a grave in Florida, his name marked in a family tree with a black triangle pointing backward to his name, a broken limb. Her husband gone for a routine surgery, his adverse reaction to anesthesia, his mad wandering into neighbors' homes. The VA housed him in the closest hospital, five states away, in Massachusetts.

I see her sacred, burning heart held out, its threads stretching the length of the coast, the breadth of the continent, and I cut away more sharply at the faith she wanted me to keep, my love of saints a kind of phantom limb, the failures of the church its lingering pain.

The mass demanded her contrition, but for what should my grandmother have ever beat her breast; through *whose* fault, through *whose* fault, through *whose most grievous fault*?

When in later life she lost the fullness of her sight, the surgeries, her prayer, did not newly-fix her eyes. She held a lenticular magnifier to the pages of large-print books, spent afternoons listening to songbirds she had drawn near to her, suet in the branch beside the screen window, her open hand resting on her heart.

Meredith S. Jensen

I Remembered What You Told Me About the Daffodils

I picked them up at the end of the road, the Youngest and their friend. Sunshine dappled their heads with the light of a too-soon spring. Perched on a low wall, legs swinging, they looked every bit the pair of teenagers they are.

Packs looped over slouchy shoulders.
Oversized hoodies,
beanies,
boots.
Faces that ripple between joy and indifference and adulthood and
childhood.

I'd dropped them off here a few hours before, their secret mission tucked behind the trees. As a parent, I asked enough questions to know they were safe. As a parent, I asked enough questions to know just enough.

Make good choices, my parents said, so I say it now.
Give me the outline,
write your own details,
fill me in later.
This is the Contract of Trust.

They loosed themselves from the wall and dropped to the tangled grass. They moved like foals on cross country skis as they loped toward the car, bones full of secret jokes. Their giggles reached the backseat before their bodies.

"Oh! I remembered what you told me about the daffodils!
There are a bunch coming up around there."

The air sparked around the words as they spread out in front of me, taking shape as a flashback from one morning's drive to school. As a parent, we teach when we can and impart what we must. As a parent, it's a surprise to see what sticks.

Naturalized citizens of the Appalachian woods, keeping memories of
homesteads that no longer stand:

Daffodils,
Jonquils,
Narcissus, all.

Flowers of playwrights and poets and presidents, Greek myths and colonists.

I turned the car toward our own sloped yard, blanketed in century-old bulbs and blooms. They've escaped across the road over time, patches of yellow tumbling down the hillside toward the river. Narcissus, always seeking his reflection in the water. Parents, always seeking our reflection in our children.

"I remembered what you told me about the daffodils."

Sheila Carter-Jones

At the Wall

I keep the body of a bumble bee on
the wrought iron table, wings thrust back as if
ready for takeoff, the abdomen bears full weight of
emptiness, holds spiny legs stiff in last grip .

It is like the cherry wood urn—small delicate creature
full of my brother's ashes that rests on my altar table.
Its round body is plump as the fuzzy black butt of a
bee squeezing home through a small hole—

D. M. Carter enters

the nest of etched names, becomes a reflection of
a young boy inside a wall with other young boys hived
in black stone. There but not there. He colonized with
V.A. war buddies who still fight sting of demons after
coming home to a hospital tomb.

For years after the war, he pushed needles full of
Viet-girl slipping quietly into tiny punctures in the arm,
swallowed the bottle and smoked the jungle weed
until his bumble bee liver turned a yellow-black shell
cracked by weight of addiction.

Living among shadows of soldiers now, I streak his name
with my finger between two other Carters. Sweaty and
invisible—kin only through incident of blood and hands
veiled by polished black that reach through rice paddy
goo. Hands could be

D. S. Carter warning,

Back away, from queen-bee-junkie-girl. Her broken
English sweet venom crawling into veins. Or, could be

D. E. Carter, private first class,

phantom soldier, still on duty; weapon right side,
watching over my hand pressed against stone
feeling for my brother's pulse. My good ear pressed
against heart of granite, listening for some adamantine
buzz to explode the honeycomb.

Sheila Carter-Jones

Senior Tennis Shorts and Other Incongruous Ideas of Servitude

1. Technique

The instructor cheers,
Yay! You got it!

2. Happy Feet

Slap, slap, slap-slap,
slap against the surface.
If she could have only run
just a slap faster and had only
kept her eye on the ball
she might have had a slight
chance of hitting it, but
even if she did the ball probably
wouldn't have gone over the net.
Like always.

3. Grave Fact #1

After the first twenty minutes
the ball is a neon streak.
Tired muscles make
a sloppy game and the best
become lousy. The lousy
become lousier.

4. Are You Smarter Than a Tennis Ball

Green fuzz.
Flash of neon.
Pat prowls. Bounces
on tip-toes like a wind-up
toy gone mad.

The ball lands in bounds.
Pat attacks. Swoosh!
Misses by two feet.
Screams, *Dumb ball!*

5. *A Case of Name Calling Before Partner Matching*
   for the Game

Sheila Brown, right?
This is the millionth
time she's asked. And,
it's the millionth time
I've told her, No. It's Jones.
Jones. Jones. Jones.

Next time she asks,
Sheila Brown, right? I say,
I think it's my skin that's throwing
you off. She remembers Jones
the next time/ and
the time after that/
and the time after that/
and the time after that.

Now she plays on Court Three
with three other white ladies and
no chance of missing the ball.

7. Good Friday Tennis

Sally serves the homemade
chocolate matzo treat.
Breaks off pieces, passes
them out to the all the seniors.
Says like a prayer to each of us,
You don't have to eat it.

I feel absolved.

8. At Love Love

Walter forgets he's holding
the unleavened bread.
On his serve, the treat
goes up with the ball.
Sally's chocolate matzo
smashes into the net,
crumbles.

Walter says, *Oops. Is
that my point or yours?*

9. Doubles Entendre

I could have been coming to the tennis courts for 100 years.
still when the big man arrives for the first time—retired,
gray haired, yet bulk of muscle—he flexes lean privilege.
now odd player out—from the sideline I watch him serve
the ball up, raises his racquet like a champ and, *WHAM*,

the ball is a bullet. optic yellow. perfectly round missile
whistling down the baseline. a straight shot, hard—burning
with intent to gain a leg up. the new guy's follow-through
is as natural a rhythm as his gendered-skin. he gets what he wants.
easy. doesn't sweat. he's so adept. besides, who can hit a megaton
bomb of a ball coming at you faster than you can see it—even
when wearing two pairs of glasses, one goggled over the other
like Elliot with cataracts, or like me with 20/20 normal acuity.

10. Match Point

We have to have a personal talk, I tell the senior Senior Instructor.
Why was the new guy put in before me—when I've been coming
to the courts for nearly a hundred years?—so to speak.

11. Serving Up the Ad in Attitude

I know what kind of player he is,

the senior Senior Instructor says.
He's a cut throat. A league player.
I knew Kelly could handle him.
She's probably the best player here.

And, he doesn't care.
I've seen him go after his own wife.
I didn't want you to get hurt.
I didn't know if you would be able
to take it.

I wanted to see if he could play nice.
This is different than league playing.
I think of safety first.
That's my main thing.

I've got 9 million dollars of insurance.
Somebody gets hurt—decides to sue,
I'm covered.
It had nothing to do
with   race.

He's the kind
won't shake your hand after a match.
My father said,
If your opponent doesn't shake,
punch 'em.
I never punched anybody, though.
You know what I mean?

Oh, don't write a poem about me
and make me a bad guy.

M. Lynne Squires

Clothing Calamities

Clothes are said to "make the man," or woman as the case may be. Regardless, I say clothes carry equal power to embarrass the man or the woman. But let's not tarry with discussions of zipper failure, buttons popping, or the errant tag emerging from the neckline or waistband. Let's dive straight into true clothing calamities.

A woman arrived at my office, seated across from me at my desk to interview for a position. I gave her a general once over to get an idea of how well she presented herself. She was dressed nicely in a skirt, blouse, and jacket. Office-appropriate attire, certainly. I could see was fidgeting with something in her lap, repeatedly reaching toward her knees. A nervous tick, perhaps, I wondered? When she stood to leave, I saw what her problem had been. She was wearing a pencil skirt with a kick pleat. She had it on backward. The kick pleat was in the front and kept falling open at the knee.

A gentleman I once interviewed arrived looking quite dapper. Chinos, shirt, tie and blazer. He preceeded me into the conference room, at which point I noticed the eight or so inch long sticker affixed to his pants leg announcing he wore a 36" x 32" trouser.

The misplaced kick pleat and the errant size sticker pale in comparison to my own clothing disaster stories.

Elastic seems to top the 'problem features' column of my wardrobe malfunctions. Although I have long learned my lesson about holding on to clothing well beyond their expiration date, that wasn't always the case. There was the day my underwear fell down in the middle of a crowded mall. In the days of the palazzo pants, I had a fabulous pair in black and white geometric print. I loved the way the silky material brushed against my legs when I walked. They were cool, both from a fashion and weather standpoint. Striding through the crowd of shoppers, I suddenly felt something odd happen around my waist area. Next thing I know, I felt my panties sliding down my legs. The elastic gave up the ghost.

I panicked. Moving as fast as possible, while trying to hold onto my undies with my thighs, I rushed to the nearest lady's room. Of course, as is the case in emergency situations, I was the farthest point from the nearest restroom. In my panic, of course, it didn't occur to me that the crotch of said panties was intact and would only allow the smallish garment to travel so far south. Thankfully.

Staying with undergarment calamities for a moment, let's move northward to the bra. Although not overly endowed in that region, I still must sport a brassiere daily. In my adult years, many mornings would find me changing clothes for work two or three times before settling on an outfit for the day. I can assure you it only takes once to show up for work in a semi-see through white shirt, with a black lace bra on underneath to learn the lesson the undergarments might need to change as well.

Shoes. I love them. I have had dozens of pairs of shoes in my closet at any given time. Sometimes when I find a pair I truly love, I buy a few pairs in different colors. When my son was small, such was the case with my Birkenstocks. Out of a dozen or so pair, I had one particular style of the suede two-strap sandal in both a soft meadow green, and another pair in a dusky county blue shade. On Mother's Day, we attended church and went for lunch afterward. We went to my son's favorite buffet restaurant. After ordering drinks, I walked to the buffet where I waited in line behind several people. I glanced down at the floor, and to my horror realized I was wearing one green and one blue shoe. If any one of the people I had come in contact with that morning had noticed, they had the good grace not to point out that I, a fully-grown woman, couldn't dress herself.

I grew up in an era where a dress or skirt even having the possibility of being the least bit sheer required a slip. Every woman's clothing store had a 'foundations' department where undergarments were acquired. So, one fine day, I was walking through a parking lot to meet a new client for lunch at a nearby café. I try never to run late, but that day I was cutting it close. As I strode purposefully to my destination, I felt a familiar odd feeling at my waist. Before it even registered what was happening, my half-slip elastic let go and the entire slip plummeted into a heap in a circle around my feet. Looking around quickly I ascertained no one was in the lot who witnessed the slip jumping ship. As I stood in a puddle of silk betrayal, I realized that my purse (roughly the size of an ice-cream sandwich) wouldn't hold the slip. A glance at my watch confirmed I didn't have time to run back to my car with it.

So, I did what any self-assured woman would do. I stepped out my garment of betrayal and went on my way.

Donna Weems

I've Got Peas in My Pocket (Song)

I've got peas in my pocket, new lettuce in a bowl.
I've got sunshine in the meadow, a garden in my soul.
Tiny leaves of sweet corn are peeking through the soil.
And pungent garlic scapes are starting to coil.

There's a nest in next year's Christmas tree.
A sunflower holds six bumblebees.

The green beans are sprouting, beets send up reddish leaves.
The soil under the potato plants is starting to heave.
I've got a garden in the meadow, I've shaken the winter blues.
I've got peas in my pocket and I've got you.

A stately praying mantis poses in the grass.
A fat round groundhog is eager to trespass.

The blackberry flowers beckon to the bees.
It's a race to harvest raspberries before they are seized,
By the bluebirds and sparrows, goldfinches and wrens.
The garden is a love letter I am longing to send.

Spring peepers sound as night falls.
Fireflies raise their lanterns, small.

I've got a row of zinnias, a garden in my soul.
I've got sunshine in the meadow, an occasional hungry mole.
I've found joy in the rain, shaken the winter blues.
I've got peas in my pocket, and I've got you.

Donna Weems

The Cheat River Beckons (Song)

Leaving the towns, and cities behind
We don't know this wilderness, or what we will find.
Norman the shoreman, welcomes us here.
His steady kindness dissolves our fear.

Imre has planned a Cheat River escape.
We don our life vests and face our fate.
We paddle canoes filled with clothes, food and tents,
And slip past rocks, with a sixth sense.

Chorus:
The trees are our brothers, the river our friend
The Cheat River beckons, the Cheat commands!

When Atilla paddles solo, he guides just fine
But with wind, rocks, and currents, he takes extra time.
Susan is a training Appalachian guide.
She also enjoys the wild wet ride.

There's a drop in the river that lies just ahead
The V in the rapid, can barely be read
The canoe bucks and rears and slides through a chute
It seems we have managed to find the right route

Bluets, ramps, fiddleheads, lilies,
Lady slippers, elderberry, painted trillium,
Deer, bear and eagles, call this their home.
Deep in the forest you are never alone.

Endurance and grit cannot be feigned.
After canoeing the Cheat you won't be the same.
Once you have paddled it and know what's in store.
You'll find yourself yearning to come back for more.

Sue Weaver Dunlap

Dear Robin,

We walk up the road to the curve and sit cross-legged under mountain
laurel, always cool, damp, write our names in black dirt glistening
with specks of shiny pyrite. We listen for cars on the big road, wonder
if someone will turn and drive down the road to Lula's Holler where
our mothers sit on the porch, talk about old times, whisper secrets.

We walk up to the ridgetop above Grandma Goode's house. We chase
butterfly dreams, plan out a day of play, no adults touch us until "dark
thirty" when we are expected back to tote water from the spring, dodge
Aunt Annie's pet copperhead resting in the cool of late afternoon, buckets
slosh back and forth with each step back to the porch to supper waiting.

We walk along dead red hills and gullies beside Highway 68, our bare
feet cut and stinging, July's heat covering us with endless sweat, no shade
of bonnets or caps for our heads, our desire to keep up with older kin waning
with each step we take, our rock 'n roll songs now like whispers, we beg
to go back, but only to each other, our secrets safe, no desire to be ridiculed.

We walk wrinkled arm in arm down to the creek, this place shrouded by adult
fears, September closing in fast, our hearts edging around dark death coming
for you, neither of us letting the words fall from our lips, me slowing my pace
to your hard breathing, resting to watch a mountain blue bird standing guard
on a low limb, fall wildflowers painting our world red and gold, a blanket. I

take this walk as a letter of remembrance because I know where you are.

Sue Weaver Dunlap

Honeysuckle Fences

In this week of the pink moon, we labored side by side at the top of the hill,
cut and pulled blackberry briers already blooming, honeysuckle vines, twisted
thick around woven wire these past five years since the day we abandoned
a new crop ground, memories of when we augured post holes, set wooden round
posts lifted by a front-end loader on the Massey 362, broke a bit on rocks too big
to dig up, measured the perfect 100-foot square plot, stretched woven wire used
in old-timey hog lots, hung a gate to keep out four-legged intruders. Lay fallow
until now, this week when we found an abandoned bird's nest hidden deep
in the vines and my husband couldn't accept it was a cold nest. He cut sweet
gum branches and built a cover. And just yesterday, we found a doe sitting
atop a nest of three kits, just shy of a few weeks old. He cut sage and limbs
and built a hutch for protection. Next day we searched for this beloved rabbit
family, no fur or innards to be found. Perhaps it was another door to our farming
life we are mourning, not these smallest of creatures who live out their days here.

Sue Weaver Dunlap

My Longest Love Affair

It began with my secret place, a thicket of small yellow pines
down below the driveway, far enough away from the house
where I couldn't be seen, just me and my dog Butch, my most
faithful friend, lying on our quilt, cloud watching, distanced

from the angry voices or the busy house, always extra people
living with us. My next love stood strong and thick trunked
in our lower yard, a sturdy old mimosa, its most important
job sheltering me close as I leaned in against the forked trunk,

my book open in my lap, ever watchful Butch keeping a keen
eye out for Daddy's return, lest he find me in forbidden ground
for a girl. That mimosa seemed to be happiest when all of us
kids gathered for baseball games on Saturday afternoons, this

special tree our second base. I remember sitting in its shade
with all the family gathered around during the last bean harvest,
each of us with a job in the stringing and breaking of beans.
A poplar grew tall and beautiful outside our kitchen window,

its limbs always beckoning me to come out and play, *climb
as high as you can, sway with the wind, look beyond the creek,
dream big,* it seemed to say, and I did, never once afraid
of falling, not until Mama buried fear into me through her own.

Now, in the short years of my life, I watch my last love affair
bending over, its branches almost reaching the ground, seasons
taking their toll on him. Perhaps the last ice storm or gusty
winds will take him down this year, but then again, maybe not.

Chris Wood

Dog Walking on Hallowed Ground
—The Historic Dunlap Coke Ovens Park

Moss blankets the ruins, beehive ovens carved out
over a hundred years ago to turn mountain coal
into coke. A legacy built by the great, great grands
of those who leisurely walk the paths.

Stormie zigzags, sniffing, listening with her ears perked.
Can she smell the past? Hear the train whistle as it pulls in
with loads of coal from the mountain? Or the clickety-clack
of the wheels rolling down the incline?

Stratus clouds hang low, reminders of the smoke-filled valley
at the turn of the century when fire in the ovens roared,
chimneys billowing. I can taste it, hear the miners shoveling,
smell the soot still lingering.

Cathy Rigg Monetti

The Knowing

The older she'd gotten, the more skittish she'd become. This was surprising, one believing more experience ought to add up to more confidence. The opposite was true, though, the wisdom of her years proving instead just how random and untrustworthy the known world is. And this was just fact. Case in point: the morning's headline news. *Student Assaults Principal; Group Storms Library Calling for Ban of Books; Neighbor Shoots Neighbor Over Barking Dog.*

It was all so much.

She steps outside for air. For trees, for birds, for her view of the mountains that wrap this valley like a deep green cloak. Her eyes train west to the high-wire ridge where sits the old cabin she and Dave built in 2006. They loved that place, spent many a long weekend there, him tending the wild lands and her doing whatever, in the moment, struck her fancy: reading, writing, collecting fistfuls of wildflowers she'd later press or paint. She'd not been up there since that last time in early COVID—the journey having somehow become arduous, and sad.

The crow is at the railing and he hops, expectantly. Top of the day, she says to the bird, and he caws and clicks, and she sees he's brought a new shiny, his latest offering in their ongoing game of give and take. She steps to retrieve it. Oh Bertram, she says, seeing it's a locket, the silver tarnished, the monogram scratched. She rubs the front gently with her thumb, and for a moment breath catches in her throat. Was that a J? Surely not. Bertram hops, okay okay, she says, and she opens the patio's side door, steps into the utility space and scoops a cup of peanuts. It's the roasted kind he prefers, and she's hardly dumped them onto the flat feeder before he flaps his wings, takes a beakful and flies off into the late morning.

Coffee. She'd like more coffee. She'd already rinsed the pot, so she considers making another while weighing the pros and cons. She could outline her week's To-Dos, that would be productive, and she shakes off the basket, lines it with a filter, then carefully measures three scoops. The pad and pen are in their spot and she brings them to the two-seat dinette by the window. She'd never particularly cared for this set but it'd come with the house and fit the space and she couldn't make a rational argument for discarding it. Never mind the cavernous wound, the hollowing ache reconstituted by the empty chair. The world was made for two. This she knew, and conditioning the heart for acceptance was called for.

Steaming cup, she sits. She takes her time. Considers. She picks up the pen and slowly, carefully, makes a perfectly round bullet. Which one is this? *Stolen from the Mackey Law Firm* it says, and she shakes her head, mystified by the joke.

She taps the pen, now, to her cheek. What. To Do. First.

Get more peanuts.

She crosses the note out immediately; she's just bought a 25-pound bag, why on earth did she start this list in ink.

Tap tap on her cheek. Tap tap nothing comes. There must be *something*—when a tap tap sounds behind her, a sharp tap tap and she turns to see it's Bertram, pecking at the slider to the patio. What on earth, she thinks, and she rises. She reaches the glass and unlocks the bolt, and he takes three decisive hops away. He keeps an eye, though, watching her slide the heavy door open; she's careful to not let the rusty edge scrape. She steps through the opening and he watches with interest, tilting his head such that in the sun it shimmers, the feathers at once black and blue and the rich green of emeralds. The big bird hops again but doesn't go in the direction of the feeder. His motion is forward, onward, his black beak lifted and leading.

She follows. He reaches the edge, the curve where patio meets grass and stops. He stretches his long body in a motion that starts with tail and moves slow along the spine until his head raises sure in gesture. It's a point, she's sure, the way his neck slips back his head, the way his beak pulses once, then twice. He cuts quick to see she's watching, then repeats. This time, he produces a click click and a long caw. Again he turns. He needs her to see.

But what? Nothing's there but mountains, the same daily mountains, layer upon layer of Appalachia's every blue, ridge after ridge pointing, dipping, curling in the way a child's drawing might, a crayon pulled across a broad sheet to make a dancing line, continuous if inefficient. Closer still is the mountain face she loves best, the rising from valley to peak of Ogle Ridge. It spreads before them an accordion unfolding as the morning's clouds throw shadows that shape-shift and change, lighting ridges, then hollows, then throwing entire swaths into darkness.

Bertram waits.

What is it, she says. What should I see?

He flicks his head again, up up. Up to the top of Ogle.

It cannot be, she thinks. You cannot know, she says. And he takes flight, Bertram does, in one grand swoop as his wings push sure against the day's quiet air in a motion that at once startles and reassures her. She lifts her own arm, her hand coming to rest at her brow and shading her eyes as she sees the bird fly high and away toward the very spot—top of that mountain—where lies her husband in a shallow cove.

She does not move, believing the bird—*hoping* the bird—will presently return and this will be done. He does not, though, and as time passes and her anger finds space to grow, she moves to the feeder, lifts its flat bed and in a wild motion throws peanuts into a wind that has picked up, now, and blows cool, the portent of a coming storm. She looks to the darkening sky, then slips back through the slider. She pulls it closed and twists tight the lock.

Damn that bird, she says.

And she goes to gather her things.

She knows the way. She's traveled this route a thousand times—Dave at the wheel, her to his right, the two of them chatting away the miles in a discourse both interesting and amiable. There is so much to see! So much to discuss. Nothing offers the color and contrast of a country road with its vast fields and tender crops, its haphazard lineup of ancient barns and gated estates. And oh, the yard art. Today, though, she hardly notices. She sits forward, hands tight on the wheel, eyes straight ahead as the wipers wipe swish-swish in time with rain that's come, lengthened, strengthened. It's a passing storm nevertheless, a summer shower; she knows this and still she finds it disconcerting.

You can do this. You can, Jules, she tells herself. You can do this, over and over.

She's not traveled this route since the day they buried Dave, in the awfullest time of COVID. Since then no one had encouraged her to come, most especially her city daughters who, when she sold their childhood home, simply would not allow her to move to the mountain alone. It had been quite a concession, she had to admit, when they agreed she could buy the small "manageable" place sitting at its base. And sat she had, not even once summoning the courage to drive this twisty road, to make the climb, to reach the summit and step out alone onto 40 wild acres filled with black bear and bobcat, timber rattler and coyote. To face the memories and sorrow.

It lay ahead of her now. She notices the rain relenting, she sees spots of sun peek intermittently from clouds laden with wet, with dark. Thick mist rises from the asphalt and she makes the turn onto the unpaved drive, a bumpy, private road that will take her the last four miles and an additional

3000 feet in elevation. The forest thickens as heavy water collects and falls from the flapping, blowing leaves, making a loud splat as her wipers wipe intermittently. She checks the clock—2:22 pm—and notes the temperature has already begun to drop. In contrast, she feels her anxiety rise. *I will not turn around, I will not turn around,* this is her chant now, a fortification.

She reaches the final turn. She braces for sight of the driveway, a short spit of a road her husband put in himself in the first months they owned the property, Dave and a tractor and a few blasts of dynamite. They'd meant to build here where there was a natural spot with contours that were gentler, flatter, but upon further consideration they'd decided to do what it took to get the best views. If that complicated the build? So be it. Complicate it did, but in the end the house was perfect, clinging to the side of the mountain as if it had been carved there, overseeing a vast meadow filled with more rhododendron and laurel and wild azalea than an artist could dream. The driveway itself required seasonal maintenance and even with the clearance of this big SUV, which she'd kept despite the protestations of her children, she wonders if she'll be able to make it to the house.

What she sees surprises her. The vertical log they'd sunk as a signpost still stands, its base surrounded by a thick mass of happy white daisies. Nailed to the front is the wide metal arrow, bent, now, and slightly askew, most likely loved by a bear in that way they like to stretch and stroke and rub against the small pines. The paint has faded but her word is still there: *Heaven.* Sitting atop is Bertram. It has to be Bertram, his head bowed, his oily feathers glistening in rain that has become soft, malleable. The crow takes flight, stays low, bobs up then down as he follows the short path's hills and valleys, as he stops to wait in this tree and that, intending to lead her on. She makes her way slowly; the grasses have grown high and unruly, and twice she has to park, get out, clear fallen branches. She's brought her snake boots, which she puts on, and a pair of thick leather work gloves and also the handsaw which Dave insisted they have in the car at all times, *one never knows what one might encounter.* It was good practice then, on these roads, even if she teased him. It's good practice now.

Then there it is. The house, their house, low-slung and waiting. The roof intact, the windows closed but hoping. She parks, gets out, shuts the Ford's heavy door. The rhododendron they'd literally built the house around has become monstrous, a statement, obscuring the steps, the front walkway, the glass door that led to the mudroom with its pine bench and hanging hooks, with its insistence that things that belonged there be collected there.

She stands at the top of the descending stairs and reaches for the railing to steady. She feels the second Mrs. de Winter, the thump of her heart, the strange prick of tears. She cannot do this, she should not do this, and she waits.

Bertram squawks and she sees he is on the roof, perched to the right of the widow's peak. No, she says, no. But he calls again, and she finds she is moving, her feet carefully ascending the wet mossy ramp. Her hands hold to the railing, and she steels as she meets it all, step by rising step—her anger at the world, at that goddamn, pointless pandemic; the unimaginable loss, the loneliness she cannot bear; the knowing this is life, her life, this is who she has become.

She reaches the top. The sky has cleared. The sun has emerged, escaped, electric it lights a vast wet world below her. The whole of it shimmers with a glory that overwhelms. She cannot breathe; she breathes so deep all of creation rests inside her. Her legs give way; she stands so sure she is sky and mountain and rock and stream. She is broken and bone-tired; she is released and free and wild and soaring. She is the beginning, she is the end, she is all that came before and all that will be and she knows she is not, she will not, ever be alone.

There is the cove, behind the row of pines, and a white mist rises as if orchestrated. It is beautiful the way the vapor lifts slowly, wafts patiently, strands curling and twisting to a music only it hears. Bertram watches this intently, his eyes round and deep yellow and trained until he breaks to look to her. They are face to face, she and the bird, eye to eye, and neither looks away. He does not make a sound, just holds her gaze until he's sure she knows. He's sure she will follow. Then he raises his wings, lifts to ride the air, and flies through the mist to the grave.

Melissa Helton

Akihi

> *—n. Hawaiian: the act of listening to directions and then walking off, just to forget them*

Do you promise to do all you can to be a good husband?

I do.

Do you promise to do all you can to be a good wife?

I do.

Melissa Helton

Karelu

> *—n. Tulu: The mark left on the skin by wearing something tight*

The wedding ring has been off so long
a stranger would never guess it had ever been there.

Melissa Helton

What Life is Like Right Now

The car bounces along the drizzly,
rutted road, splashing February slush.
The driver holds a coffee cup
in the air, her anatomy trying to absorb
the pitch and yaw of the road,
cup hovering, unspilled, just the smallest
disturbance on the surface.

Bonnie Proudfoot

Roadmap

It's not the denial of pretending
you're not listening for the phone
to ring, a text to bing, of trying not
to wait for a late-again lover
to arrive. Don't go there. It's not
like there's anything to do
or not do. Or like the universe
has picked anything out for you.
It's what you might feel when driving
back, say, from Charleston, WV,
on a strange road at night, and
you haven't passed any towns
or streetlights for miles. Here,
there's no signal, maybe you missed
a sign. Maybe you pass a roadside diner,
a neon flash, lanky shadows of men
in the gravel lot stand beside
large trucks, smoking, almost frozen.
It's drizzling, foggy, the road follows
a river, glints of water flow onto
the lanes. You wonder if your car sounds
strange, you wonder whether to pull over,
but don't trust the motor not to stall,
can't decide to slow down or speed up.
Then, an animal races across the road,
a mink? a cat? toward an oncoming car,
and you do slow down. The car's taillights
vanish, the animal struggles to its feet,
its back is certainly broken, but it tries
to return to your side of the road,
small legs scuttering, each pulling
in a separate direction. You see it gain
the median, sink into grass. It's not like
you're having a conversation
with the universe, or like this
is a roadmap to oblivion.
You know where you are.

Bonnie Proudfoot

Swagger

When he showed up in Nike running shorts and flipflops,
a beat-up 20" Stihl Farm Boss chainsaw to cut down
my dead sugar maple, 80' tall, over 3' wide at the cutline,
barely 20 feet from my back porch, I should've sent him
back to Wood County. Bare-chested, no hardhat or boots,
not a ballcap or eye protection, unless aviator sunglasses
count, dressed to crack a cold one and catch the Pirates
from a chaise. Before he yanked the pull-cord, he fired up
a fat spliff. Then I really wanted to double down, get him
out of my yard before someone got hurt. But I didn't,
because you, my friend, were head over heels, dazzled
by his slice of paradise on a mountaintop, four wolf-dogs,
a drop-anything travel trailer and jones for adventure.
He could pedal his Specialized bike straight up
a logging trail or shove a tree trunk over with
his bare hands, which he basically did, after his Stihl
was stuck, the bar jammed in the cut. The tree didn't
budge, didn't even tip or lean. You and I watched from
the safety of the porch while he pounded in wedges
and spent all afternoon whacking them with a maul,
trunk swaying like it could topple in any direction.
By then, it was too late to throw him the hell out. Isn't
that how love works? When the tree pitched over
as if he'd planned it, I paid him and he took you home,
just you, him and the wolf-dogs, where I'm sure he
hefted you over a brawny shoulder and swaggered
you into his travel trailer. You fell hard. When you called
to say he had cancer, I wasn't surprised he refused chemo,
then solid food, just hits of dope, sips of water, fresh air.
Then he gave away the bike and dogs, and you told me
how he died on that hilltop looking out at the woods.
You called him the kindest man you'd ever known.
Maybe he thought he could beat cancer. Maybe he did.
I know he wouldn't have ended it any other way.

Chiquita Mullins Lee

Dessert

Hands as cool as butter pecan gather pure snow
into a perfectly silver round bowl.
Snow is a southern surprise in the Atlanta of my girlhood.
With it comes sweet treat.
I might have been more excited than my 24-year-old mother,
grabbing her only child by mittened fingers and leading me out
to the nip in the air, the chill at my tennis shoes
squeezing freezing toes.
Have to hurry because frost is rare in Georgia, and we don't linger.
Out long enough to gather our bounty.
Flavor it with Pet milk, dash of liquid vanilla,
and sugar as white as the driven.
Sweet creamy cold on my tongue nearly brings tears to my eyes.
Tears for delicious joy.
Tears for the dearth of snow days
when snow cream, snow men, and my Mama
in a sweet mood are enough.
Not an annual ritual. Some yields are insufficient, more dirt than
snow in the bowl.
Only a drop of vanilla in the pantry. Empty bag of sugar.
Then the year when there is enough—snow, sugar, evaporated milk.
But a warning.
"We better not," Mama says, her mood creamy, but her words stern.
"So much in the air. We don't know what's in the snow."
These are days of knowing, days of questions.
Who knows what lurks in those crushing crystals?
Glaciers melt, centuries old toxins release.
Ice cores of the ancients sully an innocent age.
We dare to breathe in what we can't even eat,
surrender to conditioned corners,
hating our sweat,
craving a breeze chilled by an arctic coast.
So much still to know, so much ache for things long gone.

Who knows what teases the air in these hot and haughty days,
what sweetens our palates, soothes our losses, answers absurdity.
A summer treat we craft in winter.
A mother's love surrendered to heaven.
Hungry kisses of midnight snowflakes.
Humid breath at a slippery doorstep, a melting winter porch.
It's a salty irony.
A southern girl's fever dream.

Chiquita Mullins Lee

Why Poetry?

Because the moon is a cozy gentleman,
and the sun, a saucy tease, flirtatious at 6:30 p.m.,
daring me to face her eye to eye.
Because my own jokes crack me up
and lobster is delicious, and I still
haven't found a better word than succulent.
Because Mama made me really believe Jesus loves me.
Because dancing is mandatory,
and falling stars kiss the ground and splash
a dancing rainbow of teasing reds,
audacious emeralds, and belligerent blues.
Because a deep brown girl suffocates when silenced.
How else would I know?
How else could I hear the siren of your secrets,
your whispers that shatter the world?

Laura Leigh Morris

Best Mom

The baby's first night in his own room, Amelia checks on him at least twice an hour, clicking the monitor's button to illuminate the screen. He lays with his hands by his face, sometimes sucking a fist while he sleeps. Once, he turns on his side, and she worries he'll flip to his stomach, get stuck. Except he rights himself and puts his hands behind his head, looks like he's relaxing in a hammock on a summer day.

Amelia is not relaxed, did not want to move the baby to his own room for another few months. She can mostly relax when he's within arm's length, his bassinet pressed against her mattress, her breath mingling with his. Except she has to admit he is sleeping better than usual tonight. Though she won't say this to Claude.

After she clicks the monitor's button at 2:21 am, 2:47 am, 3:04 am, Claude says, "He's fine. He's sleeping. Like I'm trying to do."

"What if he needs me?" She's barely slept. Has stopped herself from looking more often.

"He won't."

"But what if he does?"

"He'll cry."

"What if he doesn't know he needs me?"

Claude doesn't answer.

Amelia waits, but then he snores. She wants to hit the button, but if she does, Claude will wake. Will be mad. Besides, she knows what she'll see: the baby's mouth open in an O, hands relaxed beside his face. If she were to enter his room, she would hear his tiny snores, the hum of the noise machine.

Except she can't help but think she'll see someone cutting the screen from its frame, testing the window locks. A woman who followed Amelia home from the store after seeing her baby, a woman who's suffered too many miscarriages, who thinks Amelia's baby is meant to be hers, will stop at nothing to have him.

Or the baby will somehow get hold of something small and round, an almond maybe, and squeeze it in his palm before shoving it in his mouth. He will think it's a toy, not knowing it means a thrashing death as he claws for air. Claude will have dropped it in his crib by accident, wandering the house while snacking on handfuls of nuts that Amelia finds everywhere:

in the laundry basket, on the bookshelf, behind the toilet. She shoos him from the baby's room, but Claude insists he can eat where he damned well pleases, says she overreacts to everything since the baby's birth.

Or the cat got into the baby's room, darted in when Amelia slipped out earlier, and she's jumped into the crib. She thinks the baby is her kitten, comes when he cries. Except in her attempt to keep him warm, the cat suffocates him. The baby breathes in fur, tries to push her off, but the cat is too heavy, neglected and overfed since the baby was born. He struggles while his mother lays in the next room, wanting desperately to click the button.

Or the branch on the tree outside his window will break, smashing through the roof and onto his crib. He'll die instantly.

Or nothing will happen, except the baby will stop breathing, and Amelia won't be there. Won't know that her boy is desperate for help because her husband insists that he sleep in his own room, that she not watch him.

The longer she's awake, the more ludicrous her visions: clothes falling off hangers and floating across the room on rogue air currents, landing on his face; a party in his room, confetti raining down, filling his nostrils until he can't breathe; interviews with women he invited in his search for a new mom, the right mom.

Amelia stares at the ceiling, wills time to move more quickly. She considers taking the monitor to the bathroom, except Claude will know. In the morning, he'll say, "You should talk to someone." He's said it before, doesn't understand that everything she does is for the baby. He says, "My mom didn't have those gadgets, and I turned out fine." She has no response that won't piss him off, so she says nothing.

At 4:30 the baby cries out, and she's out of bed and at his door before his first squawk dies. She turns the knob, and the cat shoots through the opening, desperate for release after being locked in all night. Amelia races to the crib, but the baby is only hungry, not gasping for air, no fur plastered to his face. She presses him to her hammering heart, whispers, "Momma's here. Momma's right here." She manages to put the boppy around her waist without setting him down, unclips her nursing bra, and he latches before she's fully settled in the rocker. She leans back, closes her eyes, feels her anxiety melt away.

Except she's too relaxed, starts to drift before she jerks awake, forces herself to sit straighter, keep her eyes open. After all her worry, she'll be the one to hurt her boy: dropping him and breaking his neck, smothering him when she falls asleep on top of him. She forgot to bring her phone, stares into the dimness, sees a onesie on the floor. Must have fallen from the hanger. Except its farther from the closet than it should be—carried by an odd draft. Amelia shivers.

The baby detaches, squeals, and she flips him, presses his face to her other breast. He makes snarfling noises until he's fully latched, and she stands, pats his butt as he eats and she paces the room. She steps on something small and hard. She turns on the overheard light, kneels, careful to hold the baby close. Not an almond. A peanut. Claude. Who doesn't listen.

In the corner, something else. She walks on her knees, leans closer, spies brightly colored paper: confetti. She presses her finger against it, and the little dots stick to her skin, glitter too. No earthly reason.

The baby detaches, looks up at her, grins. "You?" she asks, except no. It can't be. He blinks, continues to stare. She looks away first. Those eyes know too much.

She sits in the rocker, holds him to her chest until he falls back to sleep, still doesn't lay him in his crib. She keeps her eyes open, listens for scissors on the screen behind her head, the crack of a tree branch. Twenty minutes before Claude's alarm goes off, she puts the baby in his crib, sneaks back to bed, closes her eyes, suppresses the desire to click the button.

Claude sits up, rubs his eyes. Amelia presses her palm against the small of his back. Claude turns, smiles at her. "See? He did great. Don't you feel refreshed?"

Amelia nods, smiles with closed lips. When he leaves for work, she will take all the nuts from the house, ban Claude from eating anywhere outside the kitchen. She'll call a tree removal service, will pay whatever they ask if they can remove every tree in the yard by the end of the day. She will search the baby's room, find the notes she took on the other moms. She'll study what they've done right, will model herself on these lessons. Will make her baby the safest, the happiest. Make herself the best mom.

Anna Johnson Kline

Sway Me To Sleep (Song)

Winter voices unfinished work with
"I take it back" cold snaps and
rainy day tantrums
while a chorus cries,
"You've had long enough."

Every time I hear the river
Rushing that way
Pounding like a restless heart
Alongside you, I would swim away
Til downstream we were caught

CHORUS
It's springtime in Kentucky
My long, lost friend
Where the sun shines on longer days
Sometimes at night
I hear him callin'
Say a prayer for my soul to keep
Let the mountains sway me to sleep

My bark is as tough as a hickory tree
And all cuts they say will heal
Carved deep with the blade of a silver spade
Laid open a fallow field

Winter's cruel and callous
in coldhearted ways and
don't allow no cutting edge
Hard as the ground, without a sound
Our love will never fade

Anna Johnson Kline

So It Goes (Song)

The farmer scatters his packet of promises
In the furrowed dirt and
Returns the next day
And the next
To forage for dreams
to unearth.

Six hundred acres of rolling green
This dark, tilled earth is my
Only creed
Such a sight in front of me
Answers await the man who sows the seed

Crows feet smiling at the sun
The cooking and the canning have
All been done
Blessed be to God above
Our harvest he made a prosperous one

CHORUS
Mule and bridle
Plow to dirt
These hands have seen no other work
Prayer and sweat coax a work of art
From the ground on up
So it goes, so it goes, so it goes
From head to heart

There's a rattle down in my bones
I don't mind the past 'long as it
Leaves me alone
Children hear my humble words
There's more to life
Than what's carved in stone

Patsy Kisner

How Can I Help You?

The raccoon that broke
into the coop didn't
just kill what it ate. No.
It killed them all, except
the hen that hunched
in the corner, feathers
tattered, off-balance
from having her eyes
clawed out—bloody
sockets seeking.

I've witnessed an old mare
pummeled by the kicks
of younger horses,
from some instinct to attack
what's weak. I dressed
the wounds with scarlet oil,
picked the bloody scabs
so no scars would form,
then placed her in a
separate field, alone.

I've seen a coyote
carrying the limp
body of a dappled
fawn, then followed
the bloody trail—
each drop a red pinprick
upon the grass
until I stopped. What
more did I really
want to see?

At the end of that long,
hard day, bloody pools
swelled beneath my hospital bed,
but holding you close
I sang to settle your cries—
hush sweet baby, let
Mama's love keep you
warm, keep you safe,
until I can teach you
to howl.

Patsy Kisner

After

So many days
are a blur,
but I still
feel their weight

pressing
upon a heart
that has yet
to explode.

The grief has been
an icicle that
sometimes mercifully
melts and drips—

what it waters
even grows.
But then I feel
a chill return

to my bones.
Teethshiver.
I can't touch
until I find

gloves. Breath
becomes
a cloud. Words
become vapor.

It's hard
to explain
to someone
who is warm.

Barbara Lyghtel Rohrer

An Ancestry's Alchemy

My paternal grandparents lost their home during the Depression of the 1930s. I never knew them. They had died before I was born. But I was told my grandmother loved that house, that she was never quite the same after losing it. The reason for the loss: my grandfather had been ill and became unemployed. That much I know to be true. It is also true that this story has a wealthy uncle. Uncle Gil. My grandfather's brother.

Uncle Gil and Aunt Eva did not have children of their own, but they had money. Why didn't Uncle Gil help his brother? Instead, "he didn't give us one damn dime," I once heard my father say.

My mother told me how when she and Dad were first married, and she would suggest that they visit Uncle Gil and Aunt Eda, Dad never wanted to go. "When he told me why, I quit asking," she said.

"Your father is bitter," she said.

Take Care of Each Other

Dad didn't talk much about his family losing their home, but the story carries a weight that we kids picked up. You don't let a brother or sister go without. You don't let a sibling lose their home. You take care of each other.

Over the years, we did just that, lending money, lending tools, lending hands. When one of us was knocked down through divorce, unemployment, accidents, even assaults, the rest would gather around, holding the sibling up, until he or she could stand again. This is what my brothers and sisters and I did—still do—even though we may still struggle in other ways with our relationships with each other at times.

Yet, there is another side of this relationship with my brothers and sisters that did not become clear to me until my thirtieth high school reunion, when the class valedictorian and I swapped stories of our lives after graduation,

"I don't know that I could have done what you have done," she said upon hearing of my checkered career, most years self-employed in some kind of writing capacity.

I did not tell her this, but I think one reason that I could take the risks I did was because I always knew that as long as I had siblings, I would have a roof over my head and food to eat.

What Matters

I don't know why my Uncle Gil did not help his brother. I hardly knew him. And at this point, it does not matter. What matters is that in this story I recognized a mythology that shaped us. Families need to take care of their own—I doubt if my dad knew that is what he taught us. Dad was not one of those fathers who took time to teach lessons or skills to his children. He went to his job everyday. Evenings and weekends were often spent, when not watching TV, at the neighborhood saloon.

Yes, Dad drank, but he was also faithful as a family man in the only way he knew how. On Friday evenings, he took Mom grocery shopping, us kids in tow. On Saturdays, during the summer, Dad would fill an old red metal Coca-Cola cooler with ice, Hudepohl beer, and soft drinks, while Mom packed a picnic lunch in a cardboard box. He'd load us all into his old turquoise blue Oldsmobile and off we go upriver to a camp for a day of swimming. On Sundays, he took us all to Mass.

Occasionally, on Saturday nights, my brothers and sisters and I sprawled across the living room watching TV, Mom mending clothes, Dad would look around. "Coney Islands?" he'd say with a grin.

"Yes!" we kids yelled. And with that, Dad took off for the local chili parlor, coming back with a warm white box full of hot dogs in buns covered in chili and cheese.

"Those two on the left are for Barbie," he said pointing to the coneys on the end. He always remembered that I liked mine without the hot dogs, just as he always remembered when bringing home a bag of candy bars that one had to be a Reese's Cup, my favorite.

When Dad died at the age of 79, my older brother Jack spoke at the gravesite. "Any generosity we have for each other, what we have to give, comes from this man," he said, pointing to the casket of dark polished wood set before us.

And so it is: through some alchemy of ancestry, Dad's bitterness became our benevolence. My siblings and I live that grace to this day.

Linda Parsons

Blood Oranges

Not because it's pleasant, or because my family expects them, but because the oranges are pieces of eight, sunken treasure I unearth every Christmas to peel and quarter—citrus oil spit in my eyes, fingers numb, a kind of torture I keep repeating despite myself, like my grandmother cutting and ladling the same into her crowning compote dish, shy and magnified behind her Magoo glasses from cataract surgery, her blunt fingers so like my father's, whose hands I stilled in dementia, sure he had lost his plane ticket and I must, must call the airport— and for a moment I still my own hands, juiced sticky, capillaries shrunk, nails blanched, before I loosen the pith from its sunful meat brighting December's gray well—I think of my grandmother, the last of nine, who favored my boy cousin though I was the first grandchild, our shyness more kin than not, we met in a place neither sour nor sweet, a middle place never fully bridged—until winter wheels back around and I run my touch over pebbled skin, slice through, and pry out the teardrop seeds, this gold bullion mounded high to bookend her Christmas bowl, its garland of winesaps and coconut, my fingers stung, burned blue to white, so cold I have to stop now and then to let the blood and the feeling rush back until I can hold the knife again.

Leatha Kendrick

At the Edge of Everything

Last night, sun storms
            purple green curtains
sheers blowing in a solar wind
                  wavelengths graphed
across the magnetosphere—
                        I almost forgot we had one!
A magnificence
I remember seeing as a child
I remember being
shepherded to the edge
of our field, at the edge
            of our yard, at the far edge
of our small town
I remember night then, darkness
broken only by the swath of stars,
the Milky Way—I thought it was
a highway through the universe.
I remember how the green and purple
            hung and shimmered
            how the Aurora Borealis seemed
                        to flutter in the dark
            to move. I thought
of curtains as they grazed our wavy wooden floor
            of air and sunlight moving
                  through the room
                  of earth, our house
            us standing at its door
            unfelt winds streaming
            through every rock and bone.
I knew (how did I know?) everything
                              moved

spinning us, circling some center out of sight.
The Milky Way a spiral—
                    a dinner plate of bright dust
                    stars and planets flung out
                              spinning like a skater
                                   arms drawn in
                              across a black expanse of ice.
In that field at the edge of everything
          we moved, at ease in the quiet
          We stood in our cluster
                    our lifted faces catching ancient light
          We might have been another constellation,
          weather-beaten symbol weighted
          with our human stories
the Great Bear, Orion with his star dog, Cassiopeia, Aurora,
                    curtains at a window
or a surge of plasma intersecting atmosphere.
Words we grope toward to house our wordless cosmos
to bring it down and settle it around us
                    door
                    wind
                    floor
                    home.

Leatha Kendrick

Old Short Tail

He stood in the dark cube of the stall
at the foot of the ladder to the loft
where I escaped to be with the sky,
in the odor of hay, the warm musk
of living cattle, dusty air
of ground corn feed—this steer
we called "Short-Tail," the one
who'd be our hamburger come fall.

Each time I passed, I spoke to him,
caressed the broad expanse between his quiet eyes.
I loved the warm furred bone of that wide face,
sank my fingers into the shallow bowl of it.
What did I say to him? Something
like thank you, though no words could hold
the covenant we'd entered with this one—
chosen for our table—and I'm sorry
betrayed the dignity of his part
in what we shared. (None
of his half-brothers in the herd
were meant to survive, of course,
but we had less to do, we thought,
with their dying. We died, too,

we understood.) I took hold of the ladder's rungs,
free to lift myself to the hay-strewn floor above.
I swung my legs out the open second-story door,
dreamed the lowering sun in the silence
of his huffing breath, the small sounds
of his hoofs on the dirt floor. On restless days,
muffled crashes as he flung his length
against plank walls, used his wide snout
to flip the water pail

off its hook. What he wanted
I was not at liberty to give.
At dusk I swung down and
stroked him goodbye. I stood
a moment longer than made sense,
walked through unfurling air
to find Mother penned between
sink and stove, her hair curling, damp
with supper's steam.

Leatha Kendrick

Ode to Not Being in Charge

Dear weedy verge, dear wasted edge
unkempt along the sidewalk
thank you for your gift of bloom—

speedwell, field pansies, sun-
burst dandelion. Dear sturdy crown
of gold exploding in seed stars,

dear delicate faces lifted
to the light, dear blue eyes
tucked in rampant vining,

this is my letter back to you,
this is my thanks
to those who let you be,

to benign neglect
that flowers without
expectations.

Rachel Rosolina

Mamaw June

Carly's mouse hovered over the Tripadvisor link: "Foodie Ghost Tour in beautiful downtown Knoxville." It was a novel concept, combining food with the paranormal. She was intrigued. The outing didn't have many ratings, and only one goofy review—"To DIE for," said BestGrandad213—but it could just be new. Plus, it was the only option based on the openings in her schedule. The Association of Retirement Home Professionals conference was keeping her busy, her days packed with lectures, and most evenings with floor shows of the latest medical carts and digital photo frames and occupational therapist tools. Still, she wanted to see the city.

She'd been here many times as a child. Her Mamaw June had grown up inside the bounds of the Great Smoky Mountains National Park and had taken her grandkids to Knoxville every summer. When Carly turned thirteen, Mamaw June took just her—not her two older brothers—to visit World's Fair Park and the glamorous golden sphere perched atop twenty-six stories of scaffolding. She'd even allowed Carly to pick the restaurant for supper, a special occasion compared to the hand-washed baggies with white bread pimento cheese sandwiches that were their normal fare for these trips. Carly had decided on a taco place and had sweated through the salsa that came with the chips because she didn't want her grandmother thinking she'd chosen poorly. Beyond tacos, Carly didn't remember much from that trip. Instead, she could smell her mamaw's Chanel No. 5, which had seeped into every item of clothing over the years. She could picture her mamaw's papery legs sticking out of teal capri pants. She could hear the way her mamaw sucked on her dentures.

Carly clicked "purchase." She may as well have some fun.

...

The tour was scheduled to begin at 8:00 p.m. sharp in Market Square, just as the blue September dusk was settling. Carly arrived fifteen minutes early and sat on a metal bench under a tree draped with a string of lights. A young couple, hand-in-hand, walked the far end of the mostly empty plaza, and Carly could hear traffic a few streets away, but otherwise she was alone. Had she gotten the time, or even the date wrong? She'd done that once before, when purchasing a railway ticket on her only trip to Europe. She'd been so embarrassed to visit the ticket office and explain her dumb American mistake.

At 7:59, a dapper Black man holding a "Terri-fried Tours" sign walked up. He wore a three-piece suit with a paisley bowtie. Carly looked down at her shorts and tennis shoes. She hadn't noticed a dress code on the tour site. She gave the man a crooked smile. He nodded, his strange red goatee catching the amber light of the streetlamp, and stood ten feet away.

At 8:01, Carly walked over to him. "Are you leading the food ghost tour?"

He looked at her like she had two heads.

"I signed up for this tour online, and . . ." She gestured toward his sign, which he had nearly hidden behind his back.

He leaned the sign against his long legs and held up a finger. Squinting, he scrolled through a glowing document on his phone.

"I'm Carly, if that helps."

He squinted at her and back at his phone. "Ah, here you are." His voice was deep and melodic, perfect for a ghost tour.

Carly relaxed a little.

"This is kind of a . . . private tour. How did you find the link?"

She looked around. No other guests had arrived. Was he waiting on some bridal party or a family reunion? "Oh, I'm sorry! I didn't realize. I just purchased it online."

He looked her over and nodded. "Well, I guess it won't hurt this one time. My name is Sonny. Are you ready?"

"Is it just me?"

He laughed and glanced to his left, as if he was sharing an inside joke with someone. Catching himself, he cleared his throat and looked thoughtfully at Carly. "Don't worry, you're not alone."

Carly nodded, skeptical, but Sonny had already turned and was walking away.

...

She followed his bobbing walk to a hearse parked on a side street. It was a rich, sparkling purple and had been retrofitted to be open-air, like one of those awkward car–pickup truck hybrids. A pair of faux-leather bench seats faced one another in the back.

Carly buckled herself in and held her purse between her knees. Sonny sat up front and started the engine. The autumn breeze felt nice as they began rolling down the street. He pointed at the loudspeaker positioned in the back floorboard. It was getting dark, but Carly could have sworn she saw watery lines of light whisping at her feet.

Sonny's voice rumbled from below. "Welcome, folks!"

Carly peered around the empty hearse in the dimming light. Maybe he was live streaming.

Sonny continued. "We have a special guest with us today! Everyone say hi to Carly!"

Unease crept up Carly's back. A chilled breeze, like a palm, pressed against her face, pinched at her cheeks. Sonny's grin, framed by that impossibly red goatee wobbled in the rearview mirror, a cheshire cat.

"Who's gonna tell her?"

Carly's seat belt tightened.

"Oh fine, I will." Sonny pulled the purple hearse alongside the curb at the first advertised stop, Awaken Coffee, in the historic Old City neighborhood. He turned in his seat with a grin that, in the wrong light, could appear sinister. In the headlights of passing cars, though, he just looked a little eccentric.

Carly gripped her purse just in case.

"June says hello."

Just then the fragrant notes of bergamot and lemon wafted past. Chanel No. 5. "June?" Carly asked.

"Oh, apologies. Mamaw June."

The scent grew stronger.

Sonny ran a hand over his red beard. "Easy to see where your confusion happened. Technically this is a foodie ghost tour, yes, but honey, it's for ghosts who are foodies! Like your grandma here. She's one of my regulars. I still don't know how in the hell you were able to sign up for it." He shot a look at the seat next to her like someone was talking out of turn.

"Was this Mamaw's doing?" Carly asked.

He raised one eyebrow and continued on. "Now folks, we begin our journey here at this lovely coffee shop because the smells are so strong. For you newly departed, it may take a while to retrain those senses. Be patient, it will come. Now take a deep breath in—you getting notes of chocolate like I am?" He laughed, as if a guest had told a joke.

Carly had no idea what to do, so she breathed in the rich earthy scent of freshly ground coffee beans floating from the open door and the patio, where couples whispered to one another over tiny espresso cups and slices of cheesecake.

"June asked if you remembered the time you accidentally drank your daddy's coffee one Christmas." Sonny hooted in laughter. "She did that? June says you just let it dribble on out of your mouth."

Carly giggled, uncomfortable. How could he possibly know that if Mamaw June wasn't right here with them? Another cold chill. She'd missed her mamaw so fiercely since her passing a decade before. This whole time, she'd been on vacation in Knoxville? Carly tucked her hair behind her ears like her mamaw had done for her when she was a little girl.

"Ok, folks, moving on to the next stop!" He pulled down the street and made a right.

The next restaurant, Southern Grit, had a lovely patio with glowing tea lights on each table. Carly hadn't eaten dinner, since she'd assumed the tour would include bites along the way, and her stomach growled loudly at the smell of fried green tomatoes and fresh biscuits.

"Your mamaw says you just hold on. The next stop's for you." Sonny's smile reappeared in the rearview, his voice bursting from the floor speaker. "For the rest of y'all, this one is meant to bring back all those lovely memories around the supper table. Remember stewed apples and fried chicken? Why yes, Dwayne, cornbread too! Meals with family are some of the strongest memories we can have."

Carly closed her eyes and tried to imagine she was dead. To play out the fantasy, she had to fast forward through a long, happy life, where she'd found a partner and had passed in a comfortable bed in one of her company's nicer retirement homes. She pictured sitting on this exact bench seat, surrounded by happy older folks, her mamaw's thin-skinned hand in her own. She could almost feel it, the way her blue veins were spongy to the touch.

The hearse was moving again, another right and then a left onto Gay Street. Carly opened her eyes. Across the street was a familiar building: Chivo Taqueria.

"This one requires a brief walk, folks. Gather all your belongings." He cackled at his own joke then looked at Carly. "You actually should though, hon." She grabbed her purse and followed him into the restaurant. He spoke for a moment with the man behind the bar and then directed Carly to sit on a bar stool closest to the wall.

"This is from your Mamaw June," he said.

It was a duck taco with sour cherry compote. Her exact order as a thirteen-year-old who was just learning that food not boiled within an inch of its life—her mother's preferred methodology—could be world changing. She closed her eyes and took a bite. It was everything she remembered. Sweet, umami nostalgia. She remembered the heat of the salsa, the glint of pride in her mamaw's eyes, even the perfectly white peppermint she'd handed Carly between courses to cool her mouth down.

"It's still good, right?" Carly could hear her mamaw's gravelly voice and nodded. Sonny clapped his hands in delight.

...

"Most people think three a.m. is the most active time, but that's just for young ghosts. If you want a decent crowd, early evening is better," Sonny was saying.

Carly was barely listening. Instead she was holding on to swirls of perfume and the hissing sound of polyester rubbing against itself.

Their next stop was just down the sidewalk, so they continued walking, Sonny talking mostly to himself. He stopped in front of a white brick façade, the Phoenix Pharmacy and Ice Cream Parlor. After a little jazz-hands flair, he leaned over to Carly and said, "I always make sure this place is on the agenda because they love the old-fashioned ambiance and the history. Beulah tells me this place has a knack for burning down, but I try not to ask too many questions." His booming voice slid further into a whisper, "Between you and me, she looks like a bit of a pyro."

Carly was starting to like this fellow. They walked into what looked like an old soda fountain with exposed brick behind a long counter. A teenager in suspenders put down his smart phone and took Sonny's order.

Sonny licked the strawberry ice cream dripping down his thumb. "Normally I don't partake, but today seems like a special occasion. Now Terrance here really wanted to smell the triple chocolate swirl, but June ordered you this." He handed her a waffle cone with a double scoop of pistachio and olive oil. "She said you always were her adventurous eater."

Carly licked all the way around the cone. "So how many guests are on the tour tonight?" She could see the teen look at her strangely from the corner of his eye—he was probably live tweeting their conversation—but Carly didn't care anymore.

"Oh we have five tonight not counting you. June, of course. Then there's Terrance, Dwayne, Beulah, and Orby."

"Well, tell them all hello from me, and thank them for letting me crash your party!"

"They can hear you, child," Sonny cackled. "Let's head on back to the hearse."   ...

The last stop, and the fanciest, was back on Market Square. Sonny led her to the patio of the Oliver Royale.

"Your mamaw just said, Thank god she is old enough to drink!"

"My Mamaw June said that? I thought she was a teetotaler!"

Sonny leaned his head back and laughed. "She may have been, but she ain't now, honey. She wants you to order one of those black walnut old-fashioneds."

Carly sat with Sonny at a four-top that looked directly at the bench she'd been seated at alone just an hour or so before.

"June tells me your great grandfather was a still man back in the mountains. His spirits were legendary."

Carly had no idea that moonshining was in her family lore. "Is she happy, Sonny?"

"She is, child. And she sure is glad to see you. Says you are cute as a button and don't look a day over forty."

"Considering I just turned forty last week, I'll take that as a compliment."

The cocktails came in beautiful glassware that reflected the dainty strings of lights in the plaza. Carly took a long sip, and let the bourbon warm her through.

Sonny relaxed back in his seat. "I learned once that the burn you feel from bourbon, the one right here—" He put a hand to his chest. "That's called a Kentucky hug."

Carly let loose a laugh and took a mental photograph, searing the moment into her mind: the breeze, the faint chatter of living patrons, the sweet heat of the cocktail, the smell of her grandmother.

"Thank you for letting me tag along tonight, Sonny. It was more than I could have hoped for."

"Oh, it's my pleasure. And I do hope I see you again—just not too soon." He winked.

She dug in her purse for a tip, but when she pulled her hand out, beneath a couple of crumpled bills was an individually wrapped, perfectly white peppermint.

Jessica Manack

Two Weeks Late

Everyone says *a Christmas baby would be so fun*!
But you don't come. The clock ticks. 1, 2, 3, 4, 5, 6.
My mother took two weeks off work to help us out
and the days pass underutilized. But not without activity:

there's the pineapple-eating, the endless walking up
and down stairs, the membrane sweeps, the Foley bulb
and its ungraceful insertion, the bouncing on the exercise ball,
the fruitless pumping of the pump. The drinking of the juice

and the listening for the heartbeat. So many checks by so many
gloved hands. So much wondering about your face. My mother
shouts into the phone: WHEN IS THIS BABY COMING,
upset that my body wasn't cooperating with her plans,

and I wish I knew. My coworkers ask, tired of watching me
walk on the ice in shoes I can barely squeeze into.
My father calls, says I'll look better again once I'm not all
bloated. I tire of advice. 7, 8, 9. And then my brother

summons me from the prison, me, the single call, triangulator
between our parents who don't speak to one another.
He broke the terms of his probation. Looking at a few years.
We need to get his car off the street. 10, 11, 12, 13.

We need to get everything out of his apartment.
Meanwhile, you do your little two-step, constant and gentle,
reminding me that even as our space, our patience, get smaller
and smaller, we could still save a little room for joy.

Jessica Manack

Ballad of the Bells

My father brought me bells back from his trips,
so there'd be something safe to say I do:
collecting trinkets like the other girls,
not hiding from a monster in my room.

He flew away each week to fortune-chase
the way he chased each high, chased every girl.
Each airport seemed to have bells in their shops—
ceramic, place names painted pink and pearl.

I had a big collection, all the states:
Nebraska, Maine, Dakotas North and South.
See? We were super normal, have a look.
Then I won't need to open up my mouth.

And letters came home from his travels too—
from women, names and script unknown to us.
"I know you told me not to write you here…"
But once a bell is rung, there's no un-rung.

They sit on my shelf still, too full of code,
to break or give away sure to bring doom.
I'd shake them but who wants to wake the ghosts?
They stay in the museum of my room.

They taught me that we cultivate two selves:
the secret one/the one that people see.
No, I have never gone to Iowa,
but he did and we all enjoyed the peace.

Lisa J. Parker

Why Poetry?
—for Bill Brown

Because truly where else would you
cage the lion of grief if not
by a metric boundary of line,
by terrifying syllable,
by rules you cannot diverge from
or destroy the whole thing, lion
and all? Because poetry is
deadly precise: *disintegrate*
not *ruin; atomize*, not *smash.*
Because you can't get away with
using the word *resplendent* more
than once in a common sentence,
but how else do you describe that
pond bank that undulates, covered
in hundreds of tiger swallowtails
but to say *resplendent with color,*
resplendent with shocking yellow and cobalt?
Where else can you shout
resplendent, resplendent, resplendent?

Lisa J. Parker

Of Lean Winters

In January the green herons slept
high in birch branches,
or the lightning-scarred pond maple, keeping
air and limb between
themselves and the half-starved dogs from nearby
farms who trudged over
frozen fields, their frenzied barks at every
deer bed, rabbit hole,
an icy warning
of bloodied paws desperate in their digging,
and hungry snouts pressed
always searching against the hardened earth.

Lisa J. Parker

Respite: Note To a Friend Newly Grieved

I would never say to you *I know*
knowing full well I do not,
knowing the blank sheet of my understanding
is where you could fill page after page
of tiny script details of her: spokes of actual gold
in the variegated blue of her eyes or maybe
the way she held her mouth when she drew,
or none of those things.
Instead let me be quiet beside you where
the bodies of smaller things go on despite us, the birds
whose call and return, call and return, fill
the silence for a while, and because
birds don't say death or grief,
maybe knowing it would be the everything
and nothing of saying universe or ocean.
Maybe they understand the un-capturable
and choose to sing instead, an aria of condolence.
What I know is this: at first,
beneath it all is the sound of falling;
bucket to well bottom, rock
to ravine, but the body inevitably wanders
back to a surface, sometimes quarry-top and not open field,
but surface nonetheless, to marvel,
to wonder at the chipping sparrow or watch
the determined march of a fuzzy-backed caterpillar,
of all the things searching out necessity
and comfort before they return to spaces
they've carved out to close their eyes safely,
or rest their bodies in the quiet.

Barbara Marie Minney

Rainbow Blonde

Moonbows shed   great drops   of bloody brown tears   over Appalachia
somber winds   spread Judas kisses   across barren fields   of tomorrow
blind tears blink SOS   mountains bow their heads   in deep dark sorrow.

Picking daisies   off the PTSD of death   eight shots fired
by inexplicable rage   at the sight
of two women   engaged in an act of love
near Dead Woman Hollow
Rebecca Wight dead from her wounds.

Eight years later   park rangers stumble
across the bodies   of Julianne Williams   and Lollie Winans
in the Shenandoah National Park   wrists bound
throats slit   by person or persons unknown
Lollie's golden retriever   the only witness.

Hell must be empty   all the devils are here
Appalachian horoscopes   a jumble of nonsensical words
grieving ghosts   wallow in the shadows.

Please don't die   until I get there   no more running into the woods
coming out   just another tortured poet   looking to save her soul
searching for answers   without knowing what the questions are
choosing suicide   over surrender   another razor slice on the wrist.

I can't wait any longer   for the rapture to save us
for Santa to be nailed   to the cross
drifting into the storm   coming out a rainbow blonde

and that ain't no joke

clothed in   a suit of rusty armor
carrying a flaming sword of light
willing to join   in the fight
standing with   my foot   on the throat of fear.

Lacy Snapp

Sawdust Meditations

My father and I don our ear protection in his workshop as we prepare to plane a knee-high stack of barnwood for my latest project.

Sound restricted, he and I must communicate using signals. A slight nod of his head means, pick up this top board at that end. A stretch from his pointer finger tells me a rusty nail is still lodged in the wood like a tick and needs to be removed before we can plane. Five years working in the shop together has solidified this degree of me understanding his meaning without words. I take a black, magnetic wand and glide it up and down the board's length to look for stragglers. I'm notorious for missing the ones buried deep which will chip the planer's internal blade. Every time I make this mistake, future boards will bear a thin raised streak, the only part spared from the sharpness and pressure of the machine.

(I wonder, in this thought-provoking world of ambient humming, *would reclaimed barnwood be considered dead*? It doesn't grow anymore; instead, it shrinks into itself as more segments are cut off, sectioned, slivered, sanded.) Silverfish dwell in the knotted bones of the stack, gray creatures slinking away for survival as we remove more boards. For them, we remain patient—they do no harm to the wood. We unconsciously slow our ritual for a few extra moments to allow for them to seek out a new hiding place.

Layers of sawdust settle in the metal trash can by the planer and curve like sediment strata. A dense, thin brown strip left by some walnut boards from last week is topped by thick and fluffy sections of white pine dust, three times the size of any other layer in the tin. Emptying the buckets was always my favorite task as a child. That, and vacuuming out the bandsaw. I remember Saturday mornings when Dad would be working on projects, he'd give my sister and me little tasks, but they never felt like chores. I'd carefully open the lower blade's plastic guard cover and practice precision to extract each morsel with the hose, mindful to keep my fingers clear of the metal teeth.

Now, Dad and I plane away, removing layer after layer of the barnwood's outer skin. Most of it makes its way into the bin, but some escapes into the air, particles hovering like an ethereal mist. The gray boards are ground down until patches of red oak peek through. If I'm careful, and only take off so much, I can have both: subtle hints of gray gristle charm which seems to have seen so much, but still withholds its secrets, *and* that pinkish-brown grain that hasn't seen daylight since the log was first cut and the barn was originally built.

(This ritual creates an enormous amount of noise, and so much silence.)

We can't verbally communicate during the process, but even when the machine isn't running, we don't talk as much as I'd like. I attempt conversation—ask how mom is doing, the state of his garden, which projects he has planned for the week. I share tidbits of my own life so that he might offer some of his in return: the parts I don't yet know about, his time before mine intersected it. (I want to know what he was like at my age: the adventures, the mistakes, tiny details of his humanity to make me feel better about my own.) My grandfather would come to the workshop to tinker with his own projects, especially in his later years. In the finishing room, I'd compare his slow, careful method of brushing on polyurethane to my faster style. He'd never stop talking as he wanted to discuss politics, unpack the adventures of Huck Finn, or debate if a knot of wood on a mahogany board should be considered a blemish or beauty mark. (Looking back, I wish I would have slowed down a bit, disregarded the deadlines, and better listened instead of being distracted by my own preoccupations, ones that I now can't seem to even recall.) Moments of my father voluntarily doffing his guard are infrequent. He has to be in the right mood, with little worries on his mind, or have the right question asked to him. Even then, he might need a few days to reflect on my latest prompt, perhaps to recall the precise details himself after further contemplation.

Dad never scolds me when I ruin a blade by forgetting to remove a nail. Instead, he will bring me a freshly planed board and point to the streak that remains unlevel and unchanged, tapping the raised part with his pointer finger and making eye contact to watch as I decipher his meaning. His displeasure is wordless, but tender. Often, behind his cigar, there is a knowing half-smile waiting for child-like frustration to flush my face when I realize *I've done it again*. (He knows: sometimes, my hands might be moving, but my mind is somewhere else because he's the one who taught this ritual to me.)

Different species of lumber tower in stacks around the shop—our tin-roofed time capsule—and those one-inch strata sections are still hardened by their former life of being trees. In my first few months being an apprentice in the shop, Dad would use his pocketknife, the one he always has on his side, (the same one I always ask for when I don't have my own), to remove a large splinter of the aged gray top board. He'd hold the offering out to me, say, what kind of wood is this? I'd search for clues, little tellings like a color or grain pattern. If those weren't enough, I'd pick up the board to feel its weight or test its hardness. As time went on, even smelling the sawdust could reveal the species. (Not just smelling, but tasting. When I cut enough wood, the sawdust particles interact with the air I breathe. I cut cedar, and taste cedar. It's bright, sharp. It embodies that bright red-orange color.) These palpable markers make the qualities of wood something to count on, to trust. Red oak is red oak. Red oak barnwood, encrusted in gray, is still red oak if you plane it down far enough. It's a hard wood, dependable, with unique grain character streaking across each board, sure to not disappoint. Some people see knots as blemishes. But to us, knots are one-of-a-kind. Knots mean a tree was happy enough to sprout a branch. When one of us uncovers a knot of note, we will slow down enough to point it out, lock eyes, and shake our heads in wonderment.

(I wonder, if some consider wood to be dead after it is cut off from its roots, *why do our interactions with it bring so much life*—busyness, through craft, and our own understood layer of intimacy?)

Since my grandfather's passing, I've faced the unavoidable guilt attached to realizing I should have asked more questions. As children, we can't comprehend yet what a gift it is to have elders, how those creased bodies are the keepers of stories. We don't consider where that knowledge goes when a person is no longer living or realize that it might be buried as layers of memory within the people nearest to them. My dad is now the closest embodiment of his father. He's the one who could best recall the details, translate the grain patterns, make sense of the knots. Maybe my familial excavation is now twofold. As I ask for splinters about my grandfather, secondhand scraps to treasure, layers of my dad will inevitably be attached. To better know one is to better know both.

In the workshop, metal trash cans hold what cannot be stacked— sawdust fluffy or dense and everything in between. When I empty the bin into the gravel parking lot outside, I can remember the finished (or half-finished) projects each layer represents. This exists, too, in the mound of powder behind the chop saw, which a few pulls from the vacuum will reveal. My time in the shop consists of frequent, small revelations: silverfish making an appearance to glisten in the light before hiding again, splinters carved off so a board may be named, grain faces peering out for the first time in decades if I plane down hard enough. But there will always be those strips missed by the blade, secrets that take a little more time to wear down, a bit more careful sanding.

Jane Hicks

Blood Remembers

The girl enters the trees, feet bare,
curls afloat in lilting breeze.
The wise woman's daughter carries
baskets and bottles to gather bounty
of orchard, thicket, and forest floor
while the mother steeps, brews and dries
their foraged trove. An oaken stump
catches water to heal warts—
tree water, caught between,
neither earth nor sky water.

She lowers her baskets,
retrieves a corked container,
catches sight of a sun-brown, doe-eyed face,
coal tar hair, golden earrings. She stares to scry,
envisions flames, a guitar swirls a song,
vague memory, branches clack in rhythm,
song pricks her heart, song of a heart pierced by love.
She kens this, though not apprehending the words,
sways as the wind sweeps through.
A nut plops her mirror, ripples transform ringlets
to slow serpents, her face to wrinkles.
Spell broken, she gathers the water,
takes up her baskets,
moves into welcoming woods.

Jane Hicks

Luke 1:39-56
—After a Statue attributed to Master Henirich of Constance

We are the talk of Kerem. At the well,
the market, after temple, the house help
beset by questions. The dumbed priest,
the crone heavy with child, the kinswoman,
young and radiant as her child, too, grows within.

We love our mistress, never whisper in mirth
or slurs. I testify how the old one's child leapt
in her womb at the coming of his wombed cousin.
How the young one did glorify the Lord. We never
speak of the women's room or how the old one aches
her back with a pain no potions, pillows, or prayers
can ease. Her time comes and I worry
for the tear of weakened muscles and crack of brittle bone.

The young one calls often for the chamber vessel,
her son lies low on her. I watch and wonder
what these women who carry the weight of this
world think and ponder in prayer. I hear nought
but the worry and fret of all women as their bellies
wax with each moon. They eat, rest, and sew
garments for the boys they bear. I would hear
the old priest explain, but for his disbelief
struck dumb. I believe God, the Spirit of the Great,
dwells among us, borne in these women.
I serve them to serve God. How could I speak
of such at the well? I pray for them all,
keep these days in my heart.

Sara Henning

Lessons in Water (1987)

I couldn't stand their tirades, those hussy slash pines
and their balsam moaning. All summer, they belly-ache
their raw mint stink at the chain link edge of Cedar Creek pool
like any second-grade girl mouthing off to her mother.
The pines remind me of Brach's Star Brites,
little planets fished from my grandmother's pocketbook
summers I longed for hits of menthol I'd taste again
in my first cigarette, that heady beauty burning like Georgia summers—
grandma in her sapphire one-piece resting her eyes
on vinyl strap chaise. We'd picnic on Oscar Mayer cold cuts,
Sunbeam slicked up with Dukes mayo, Cokes fished
from an Igloo stashed in the trunk of her Toyota Corolla.
In the backseat, I learned to Tetris myself between
seahorse pool floaties and Kmart beach towels.
Aunt D drove us the mile from grandma's, where we waited
for dusk to sweet-talk its way through the pool umbrellas,
sunset upstaging their red sheen with its glamour.
Love was grandma sucking her teeth as my aunt
threw me into the deep end. It was as if the holy ghost
entered me as I thrashed and wept, belly of the pool
thrumming with wish pennies, someone's naked Skipper doll,
my body an infinity mirror reflecting the flashes my life
had barely bloomed into: Two-year-old calling
for her dead father, four-year-old eating raisins, those sweet
plump bruises, out of a box of Bran while her mother
slept off her sorrow. Which incarnation was I, hitting down
just to rise, epinephrine turning my blood to stars
until I broke the surface? Somewhere, a tornado siren.
The lifeguard whistling his rain call, no camouflage
when clouds bruised up. Soon, I learned to give myself
to water, its bluntness I hated until I longed for it.
Water is no liar. It kills us because it lives in us. Such intimacy
makes it dangerous. When I picture my organelles

in their bubble bath of cytoplasm, blood flushing my face
as I run up a flight of stairs, I'll flash to those dog days
when I learned to tread the deep, to hold my breath as I kicked
and stroked, to assume the mind of a seahorse, a god, a girl fool enough
to believe she could master anything. I'll think of my grandmother,
water in her lungs when her cancer came. Even now,
I catch myself watching mosquitos trawl my neighbor's porch ashtray.
It rained weeks ago. He's mean as a snake but he's still dying.
I am miles from Georgia, miles from the self who believed
in miracles. But the mosquitoes? They slip their eggs
like secrets beneath the water's skin.

Sara Henning

Anxiety (2023)

—We who would see beyond seeing
see only language, that burning field.
—Charles Wright, "Looking Outside the Cabin Window, I Remember a Line by Li Po"

If God reaches into me, His lumbrical muscles tensing as I count my breaths, was I born to walk through the shadow of death? Once, I carried the secret of my radiance, a matchstick in my chest, its head glazed with potassium chlorate, glass powder's unrequited kiss. I'm six, thunder's timpani assaulting the Richway parking lot off Tallassee Road. A storm slashes the sky. It kills the lights. Rain lacerates asphalt as I stare through the exit's door. And God is here, as mother said he always is, touching me with the flame that started the world. I know the world is ending. I bury my face in my mother's acid-washed jean jacket, my chest moving under the blaze I've learned to call breathing. I am not Chicken Little. My life is the sky falling. In my twenties, I live with a man off Standard Oil Street. I can see railroad tracks from my bedroom window. I sleep through the sounds of engines churning, rust and slip of each driver in constant motion, graffiti's syntax rushing the metal the way everything bleeds at the same frequency, my body or his jealousy ricocheting off our walls, his threats cutting the air as if it were my skin: *I'll kill you if you cheat on me.* I confuse *possession* for love. When I move to South Dakota to escape him, ice grafts to grain silos. Ethanol plants rise from loamy glacial drifts like monoliths. Snow closes the interstate. When I breathe, a cold I've never known burns my lungs, a burning I rise through like I do that night in Richway, like I do every time that man hurt me and called it longing, my heart's engine snapping its mounts. Even now as I hold my chest, God in my body, phone between ear and shoulder, I stagger downstairs. My doctor repeats anxiety attack, repeats breathe. If my heart is a burning field, let the dormant flung seeds of my life blaze open, speak the language of blooming. If wildflowers, not fear, muscle up from my organs, if their roots and rhizomes thrum through my bones as I lay among them, I'll ignore the falling sky. I'll inhale, petals flaring elusive as raw silk. For once, someone else can catch the moon and stars as they breach the earth's surface, shimmering like silver, rapturing asunder the whole blown ecstasy of heaven.

Leigh Claire Schmidli

Read the Sky
—novel excerpt

We moved through the night like it could hide us—even if there was a God. Especially if there was a God. We smelled of muck and moss, every inch of us thick with the rain. Jeans lay heavy at our hips, cold on our skin. My blouse held to my waist like a darling. Murphy started the old Ford and we crept along the puddled gravel, fog catching the head beams and scattering their light to a lousy halo. Murphy still hadn't fixed the heater, so we could only do what we'd done all season. We flicked on the radio. I dug the Camels from the lining of my purse, lit one for the both of us, and we passed it back and forth. We were slow about it, savoring, Murph even more so, making me wait.

...and all through the wee hours, the DJ was saying. A bass yelled out, electric, crackling from the worn-out speakers. On his wide steering wheel, Murphy did the drums. He was letting the truck coast along, the cigarette a stub now hanging at his lips. And soon it'd be time for the opening lines. Murph nodded at me and pointed, like the lead of a band, calling the next solo. I nodded back. We each felt sorry for tonight. This was our way to say it. His one hand kept drumming, the other pointing, and I stole back the smoke—a long last pull. I came in at the chorus. All about *the nighttime. Using up the stars.*

...

Sundays, we mouthed hymns. Robed in gold from neck to ankle. Sister Jane in our heads. *Stand tall*, she'd say, *tall as the corn on a blue horizon*, and in the raised pews of the choir, Jacob Murphy and I, we stood tall. Our shiny buttons were fastened to the tip-top, robes starched by our mothers. And with our mothers, even our daddies, we joined arms for the Father's prayer. We were kids who answered to the names of Saints and chosen-ones. True enough, Sundays we were golden.

Evenings, Murphy picked me up. His Ford idled in the drive—*Dusty* he called her—black finish fading brown at the hood. Under a growing dark, a pitch of stars, we rambled through the flatlands, our aim the overpass. That interstate route, built high and wide—it rose past farms and vacant county roads. When we walked under its bridge, our feet stood on quiet dirt, hardly traveled. But above us, the hurry and racket of distant cities kneaded the pavement, adding another layer of percussion.

Because below, a whole troop gathered. They had scratched guitar cases and drumsticks in jeans pockets. Names like Paul and John and every kind of Mary, they knew how to put psalms to music. They could sing *Alleluia*. They sang *Glory, glory*. Except at the highway, voices raised to other purpose. Spray-painted concrete. Six-packs already started. They pulled from truck beds and trunks, making anything an instrument. A toolbox, a paint can, wooden crates with corn silk caught in the slats. Against the corners of the underpass, the music thrummed. *Keep rollin'*, the walls echoed, *here I go. Start me up* and *on and on*.

We all took hold of sticks and strings. Hands and thighs. And the offer of a hand—many I made, many I took. Just the ghost-gray of moonshine, the right amount of hazy. No whole in mind, just this chord climbing, tip of the tongue. This verse, *darling*, calling us home. And it wasn't always beautiful. It wasn't always sweet. Sometimes, clumsy and rough and loud, we had no idea what we were doing. We broke strings and grew hoarse. We bit our lips, chafed and bled. But hell, we all tried.

Always a meek one, Murphy never offered his hand at night under the highway, but he came up with constant compliments. He told me that I sounded *real as vinyl*. He liked to say I was *the next Janis Joplin*. He used the word *flair*. Me, I liked that he could tune his guitar to fit anyone's singing. That whatever the song, he knew all the words. The calluses on his hands looked the same, whether from farming or strumming—proof to me that both could feed us. I never started a beer without first tapping my can to his. *Here's to the harvest*, he'd say. *Here's to the next Janis*.

...

Murphy reached for the volume and turned it down enough for my voice to rise above the bass line. "That's a nice flair." He nodded along. "Keep going."

He layered his words with more sugar than usual. My voice must've quieted the nearer we got to the farm. Even from a distance, we could see the house. It rose above the fog, kitchen lights ablaze, and little by little, Mother's shape stood out against the orange glow, waiting for me.

When at last we curved up the drive, Murphy's chatter had veiled the truck windows. He cut the engine, then wiped at the glass, peered outside. "We're late, Beck, real late. I can go up with you, take some of your Ma's heat."

He hadn't made such an offer since the first night he drove me, when he parked in our lane and grabbed the door handle. Aiming to escort me to the house, tip his cap to my mother. But I didn't want him to be like that. *No*, I'd told him, *leave the motor running*.

From then on, he kept the gear in drive, the radio playing, loud. We parted ways with a nod, lyrics giving the goodbye. In truth, this night was different. We'd never been welcomed to the wee hours. We'd never been out in such a rain. We'd never said things like we'd just been saying. But I hoped this night could end like all the others.

"Oh hell, Murphy." I shook my head and leaned across the seat, turned the ignition. Old Dusty rumbled awake; the speakers hissed with sudden sound. For now, we would say no more, static sending me on my way.

...

Of course the whole county knew Mother, knew the violet rosary beads that wound around her arm. The pewter Jesus and His cross often peering from beneath her sleeve. But even more so, they knew her gift.

Once she married Daddy and his farm, Mother took charge of knowing the floods and the droughts. The late frost and the early heat. Even the locusts. At dinner's end, she stayed at the kitchen table with notes she'd made through the day, scribbled on empty seed packets or in the margins of Daddy's newspaper. There were clues she couldn't ignore—like the color of dawn, trees bent in the wind. The way sparrows gathered or cried or disappeared. At night she put it all together, a final record of the weather set down on that day's calendar page, torn from a thick pad on the wall.

A page for each day, she kept the calendars from every year of her marriage, studied them and bound them. Then in a drawer, deep and long, where most women would've stored their potatoes, she stacked the patterns she found. Everyday at breakfast, Daddy asked about the likelihood of sun, the possibility of storm. When he got chipper from too much coffee, Daddy boasted. *Better than any Almanac.* Without even a glance toward her potato drawer, Mother gave her predictions. Like she was channeling that Old Testament God who spoke, giving promise and punishment, through the weather. And when I was a child I felt safe, knowing my mother could tell if the wind would rise or the clouds would part. Maybe she would be our Moses. Our Noah. Our peeling white barn, an Ark.

But the time came when Mother pressed a slicker into my arms and I began to refuse it. Preferring Daddy's old flannel, a boy's borrowed sweater, or nothing at all. I wanted to get caught unaware. To scramble for cover in a ditch. Wind-raw, from cowlick to boot heel. I pictured stealing away to the beat of windshield wipers. Like Janis Joplin would've. Janis and Bobby McGee. Hitching rides cross-country, playing harmonica through a downpour. Living from one riff, one horizon to the next. She didn't answer to any place. She didn't belong to anybody.

...

At the porch, I waited for the radio to fade with Murphy's headlights. I tipped back my head, looking for those clouds that could stick around, for those lightning flashes that could show up, even miles from their storm. They could reach over whole towns, from the steeple to the furthest field. But I found none. Just a moon, yellow and fat, trying to skirt through the mist.

When Mother saw me there, my hair in wet cords, my shirt soaked and limp, she went to the closet and returned with a towel. The kitchen floor creaked as she shifted, waiting, the towel opened, ready to wrap me up.

"The thunder came early," she said. "It gave plenty of warning, Rebecca. You must've heard."

"You wouldn't understand, Ma." I skimmed past her arms and the wide-open towel. "We followed the thunder."

I kept moving toward the living room, toward the stairs.

"At least dry yourself," she called, and the towel nipped my back, then dropped to the floor. "Rebecca Ann," she insisted, and I paused at the threshold, leaving the towel where it fell.

"Turn around here, girl."

"I'm right here." But I still held my body as if I were going. I fixed my eyes toward the living room, dark but for Daddy's easy chair, the gray vinyl grabbing all the moonlight it could. Daddy was already upstairs, certainly asleep.

A click-click came from behind me, her glass rosary beads. A ritual of hers to wrap them each day at her wrist like bangles. She twirled them this way and that—when her hands were empty, her head full. Or when her words were about to spill.

"Never mind this weather sent your cousins to the cellar. Never mind your uncles shuttered the barn. It ain't just a God-forsaken hour and you got school. It ain't just that. You're taking on a larger habit. Always with that boy. Always up against your bounds. You can't never stay still." Click-click, click, the beads snaked and spun. "I can read you, you know."

My fingers went to the collar of my blouse, worrying a loose button. My eyes followed the moon. Its glow. Two Pabst cans winked, toppled on the cushion of Daddy's chair. Three more glinted from the carpet. Daddy's seat still veered back in the reclined position as if the chair itself had enjoyed those beers and now lay collapsed in its own deep sleep.

"I see Daddy got off to bed." I turned my head so she was sure to hear me. "If someone around here can read me, Mama, I believe it's him."

I left her there, not looking back, my wet soles shrill against the floor. Upstairs, I pulled my door tight, started peeling off clothes. My hand went to my bare belly and pressed softly. I let my fingertips stay a little before pulling the hand back—like it could give me away, like someone would see. These hands, their notions of mothering.

Only Murphy knew about me. There was no father to speak of. Not one of those boys did I want such ties to. And Murphy kept the secret, but my body kept heralding the news. Another month's lack of blood, my angles plumping. Jeans pulled tight at the seams. And my hands, this way they drifted to the slight rise at my middle and perched there, ready.

Sure, a mother takes notice. And I often wondered if mine knew me. From the guitar-toting idols I pinned on my walls. The radio, hung from the bedpost, always pulsing. The night-rumpled sweaters I discarded in a pile, their incense. Grit and boy-sweat and ash. But I would not believe that Mother read my body now—whatever its wants and follies—like she could read the sky.

KB Ballentine

Broken Images

Do you hear the dark flight of crows
across the dew-fogged path that forks, (then forks some more)
before the smoke and ash rain down again?

A lament, an elegy for light (more light)
that cannot breathe, escaping from the cusp of stars.
Do you hear the dark flight of crows?

The wren-song of a morning's bliss collapses
as you set your face to work in cubic squares,
and smoke and ash rain down again.

Echo-soundings of your exiled spirit,
your dried-up bones and shriveled hope
hear the dark flight of each, of every crow.

Wrangling monsters as they gorge
your nerve, your heart, and will (they will).
Smoke and ash rain down again.

A hymn of wings, of light denied,
chaos swallowing the horizon's edge.
Do you hear the crows, their dark flight
just before the smoke and ash rain down again?

KB Ballentine

Palace of Memory

—I had no idea what would become precious. –Megan Wilcher

I had no idea my dad lost his job
the day of my wedding.
Was I so consumed
by the drama of white satin
and the man waiting
at the end of the aisle that I forgot
to notice anyone else?
No one said a word—just waved me off
with wild bird seed in my hair,
marriage spiraling faster than Dad's job.

These many years later I watch my dad
    as he struggles to breathe.
His shuffling step
        to slump into a chair
is still the man who held me
    in his arms, who rescued me
from drowning.
            Who helped me pack
    and move back home.
The loving parent in him still wants
        to protect me—his little girl
even though I'm more than half a century old.

I want to keep him here with me.
    I want to notice each breath
he takes and listen so I remember
                        the last one.

Sheree Stewart Combs

Blues

Summer Blue

Sapphire eyes turn to hazel. Somber days morph into joy. No longer a lonely woman, my baby blues lose their sadness. Bluesy voices moan to us from the stereo as we moan to each other in bed. The click of a lighter sparks a cobalt flame, followed by a long, satisfied inhalation, his hand still on my breast. Smoke plums out from the tip of his cigarette. Lady sings the blues no more.

Bluegrass music pours out of the radio as we journey through the Blue Ridge Mountains in late June. Smith Mountain Lake's gunmetal water laps at the boat we rented. Union blues still haunt Jamestown.

Murky teal water flows in Carr Fork Lake. We honeymoon on the lake for three years in a cottage nested against a steep mountain. Watch stars fall from the midnight sky. No need to wish upon a star. Our dreams thus far have come true. Until we dream of babies.

Moody Blue

Months pass. I bleed each month, bent further down by despair with each reminder of my body's failure to conceive. Couples we know birth babies, one after the other. Baby showers. Blue sleepers. Pink gowns. I dream of babies dressed in white, with cherub faces, fat, soft lips, cornflower blue, or liquid green, gold-flecked eyes. Their curls gossamer between my fingers. Breath sweet with milk. Sprigs of bluebells bloom below the neckline of our daughter's dress. Navy shorts graze our yellow-haired son's chubby knees. I watched these babies play in my husband's eyes the day we wed.

I see a fertility specialist in Lexington, three hours away, the spring before we leave the mountains. A cloak of sorrow envelopes me for six months prior to the move. The mountains formed the backdrop of my life for twenty-eight years. The home I grew up in backs up to a mountain on Blair Branch. I know the mountains like my own breath. I've drank from their streams, scaled their boulders, and waded their creeks. My footprints are forever engraved into their paths. I can't imagine a life outside the cradle of their arms. I'll be stripped of their safety when I make my way to level land in the bluegrass. It's grass tinged with blue, perhaps only in the imagination.

The cerulean sky stings my eyes the day we leave. The sun's radiance obscene on this life-altering occasion. I look for my grief to eclipse the sun, clothe the earth in darkness, and cause the stars to fall. Or, a tsunami to rise up and wash across these peaks. The mountains wail "Please, don't go," as I drive out of the holler, across Rockhouse Creek, and up Garner Mountain. "Why must you leave?" A mandolin mourns from the radio. Tears trail down my cheeks. The coral blooms of the Apple Roses along Highway 7 wave good-bye.

Midnight Blue

The move brings us to farm country and closer to the fertility clinic. I tried to strike a bargain with God. If I leave the mountains He'll give us babies. God's heart aches for a woman who thinks she can barter with Him. A woman who believes the sadness she wears as a second skin will soon be replaced with a blue-eyed boy or girl.

The mountains remain draped in melancholy. Like God, they see into our future and know this quest for babies will leave our hearts in ruin. Six years of darksome days and tear-filled nights. The world goes bleak, painted in strokes of dark stone, bleeding into black.

The baby conceived in year five dies six weeks into pregnancy. My husband pushes his grief down and keeps me tethered to the earth. He wraps his limbs around me when I become trapped in a nightmare of having been separated from our toddler in a store. Gunshots ring in my ears as I scream, "Hide, Jussie! Hide!" Jussie—short for Justina—the name we chose for a daughter.

Infant clothing, like tiny ghosts, greets us from the back of a closet. My baby spoon and pink rattle console each other in a dresser drawer. Blueprints for a cradle go back inside the bottom of the old trunk. A stack of walnut, milled from a neighbor's tree, gathers dust in the attic. We'll never watch a baby sleep inside those smoothed boards. The promise of a newborn to rock in the La-Z-Boy vanishes into blue mist. *Six months same as cash.* We finish paying for the rocker two months after the baby died.

Elaine Fowler Palencia

Mama's Bedroom

Under her cherry red satin
feather comforter
Mama and I snuggle
napping away
the long afternoon

Windows glow white
with winter cloudlight
furnace heat stirs
dust bunnies
under the bed

The dressing table
is a Sinbad bazaar
of screw-on earrings
face powder, coins
playing cards
April Violets perfume
almond-cherry hand lotion

In her closet
a velvet evening coat
and a round hat box
of love letters
whispering
single
      elsewhere
            before

She sings me to sleep
Go tell Aunt Rhodie
Go tell Aunt Rhodie
Go tell Aunt Rhodie

The old grey goose is dead.

Elaine Fowler Palencia

The Vampire's Lament

Night-shifting beside you
in hospitals and all-night diners,
driving the late buses and trains,
we do not wish to harm you
but only to see another sunset.
Being undead does not lessen
the fear of extinction.

Few of us chose the life
but rather strayed into it
lured by injudicious love, curiosity,
a thoughtless coupling.
(Free will is so theoretical,
often a mere post-hoc explanation
for the path a life takes.)

When, on a winter's night
we gather like a storm cloud
against the shadowy ceiling
of some abandoned cathedral,
our fusty capes furling
and unfurling with belonging,
our dark hearts smile, as yours would,
because we are not alone.

Who can give up community?
Comfortable with your sins,
cherished by your own kind,
who among you would have the courage
to shatter the rose window
and fly toward the oblivion of dawn?

Elaine Fowler Palencia

Beneath

Rippling like a lumpy chiffon curtain
the juvenile snailfish,
genus Pseudoliparis,
deepest-swimming fish
ever caught on camera,
glides five miles down
across blackwaternight
in a trench off Japan,
a look of mild surprise
teasing its snub-nosed mug,
like deep-buried family
secrets that never thought
they would be discovered
in dusty county archives,
handwritten records
tucked into lost Bibles,
abandoned graveyards,
census records from rural Idaho,
where none of us ever lived:
the extra wife and daughter
an uncle never mentioned,
a great-uncle's stay
in the state asylum,
an extra child living
on the grandparents' farm,
the infant brother I never knew,
all thrown off the dock of the past
in tubs of concrete.
Now they are stroking
for the surface
against the hydrostatic pressure
of family denial. Smiling,

ready for their closeup,
they whisper,
Hi, there.
Look down.
There are more of us.

Karen Salyer McElmurray

All the Mothers

Holy Mother

When I was little, I believed in none of the church-god faces—gray beards, crowns of thorns. I dreamed of mermaids, of islands, sand the color of garnets. I dreamed of camels and deserts. Sometimes, when it rained at night, I dreamed a holy woman came and sat on the edge of my bed. She smelled like frankincense and myrrh and something else I could not yet name. A woman-scent, fierce and lonely.

Granny

Strong hands wringing out dish rags in a metal pan. Skinny knife blade and a ruby red beet. Scrub brush and linoleum floor. Broom. Hoe. Well chain. Bucket. Feathers plucked from a fresh dead hen. Calluses. Raised blue veins. Steady beat of a fork in egg white. Meringue that tasted so sweet. Finger pointing out back to the smoke house. Fingers making three neat parts of a braid. Finger touching eyes that wept. One finger licking and a book's page turned. Read me a story, I said, and she did.

Lineage

Beck was my great grandmother. Her daughters were Pearlie and Opal. Pearlie's daughters were Irene, Ruby, Ruth, and my mother, also Pearlie. I recall a little about their lives. The well behind my granny's house. The smoke house, and a garden that stretched forever. I remember a dark room in my great-grandmother's house and sweet smoke from her pipe. And I remember the hush of all their secrets. My mother's monthly periods were heavy, and my granny whispered behind her hand about a woman's curse. When my aunt Ruby miscarried and tried to kill herself, my mother and my aunt Ruth fed her black coffee, walked her and hushed me out of the room. What I don't remember, I imagine. I imagine the giving birth. I imagine my granny, my great grandmother's hands massaging her belly, trying to gauge the hours until my mother's head crowned. By the time I was born, my mother was in Kansas, with my father in the air force. My father tells it this way—as she was giving birth, her voice carried down the hospital corridor. I want my mother, she called, her words taking flight. Pain had wings. It traveled the miles back to Kentucky, found the hands that knew how to comfort.

Birthday

It is my tenth birthday and all that day I can taste a cake's sweet icing. All day I say to her, I know there will be a birthday cake. I know. I know there will. Her hard-soled slippers march past me in the room where I sit, waiting. I know there will be a cake, know there will be mother-love. Just keep right on knowing, she says. She slams the door to the bathroom in the hall, and I hear the water running. Hours pass.

Love

She wanted to be there for you, my Aunt Mae once said about my mother. *She wanted to be there but she couldn't.* I know this is true. My father divorced her and she moved back home. She sat in a chair by the window and watched the world go by. The world picked me up and I rode on past.

Son I Surrendered at Birth

In the dream, I am sixteen again. I am swimming under water, trying to rise, but my huge belly holds me down. Water fills my mouth, tasting of silt and mud. My water broke hours ago, but in the dream, my son won't leave my body. He makes himself small inside me and waits and waits. In the waiting room, my father kneels to pray. A hundred miles away, my mother hasn't seen me in five years. She never prays. I dream of hands, fists closing tight. My son floats out of my body and afterbirth trails between us until he disappears.

Friends Who Have Mothered Me

Vicky, with her poems and her twelve string. Pamela, who I call so often she tells me she can't listen any more. Carlyle with her house in the woods. Wendy, who tells me my voice needs to blossom, a wicked and terrible bloom. Gwendy, who pours me one more glass of wine and gossips about all the women she knows. Marcella, who draws Tarot cards and sends me my fortunes. Prentiss, mails me photographs of flowers. Cindra, who sends me scented oils and finger puppets to make me laugh. Lorraine, who refused to try to fix my broken heart.

Pearlie

Lost in an Alzheimer's dream, my mother's arms were stiff and never touched me except for a pat, pat, pat. A hesitant welcome when I visited her again and again.

Mountains

In my mother's nursing home, a blind hundred and ten year old woman named Goldie used to look out over the tables in the dining room and say, *lord a'mercy, what they done to them mountain tops.* And I know she was right. I'm sixty, and I ride the highways to Kentucky whenever I can. As I drive I see the sawed off tops of mountains. I see the interstate that went through Paintsville and took the little town called Hagerhill where I used to live with my paternal granny. I drive past the house where my mother lived those twenty years of lonely and I see a car lot that's gone in across the road. When I visit in summers, I drive the old roads that are still there at night so that I can pull over in the dark and roll the windows down and listen to the sounds of tree frogs and locusts. A whir, a song, a spell like a mother's voice.

Gibson

When I am ninety I hope I will remember Sunday mornings at the church house in Van Lear. I hope I will remember how a woman named Mary Ruth offered praise. Mary Ruth had rough cut bangs and long gray hair she flipped over her shoulder as she picked up her Gibson and buckled its strap on her hip. She sang the same God songs every Sunday, but I hope I will remember a morning when the words were different. I was twenty years old and I was leaving home, heading out to make something of myself, something shiny as a brand new dime. That day she sang a song about home. *When the roll is called up yonder.* When I am ninety I hope I will remember Mary Ruth's sad gray eyes. I hope I will still imagine the roads she might have wanted, the songs in high school auditoriums, the songs in juke joints she could have played if God had approved. I hope I will remember how words slid out of her 'O' of a mouth, traveled down the aisle, a sad balm. Words settled in the palms of my hands. I hope I will remember how her songs mothered me on all the roads I took, away and away.

Dana Wildsmith

Not Writing

Not writing when the words are waiting
is like losing a crown on the side of your mouth
where you always chew the hard stuff—
loneliness in a cramped world,
chihuahua-sized injustices that bark like rottweilers,
how to put your own oxygen mask on first
when folks you love are suffocating.
Meaty chunks of possibility keep sliding by habit
to where the work gets done,
but then you catch yourself. Not yet.
Nothing in that space but jagged shards
of time lost to demands. Don't go there.
It hurts every time you touch what's missing.

Dana Wildsmith

Why I'll Never Be Famous

Mama died, but her four cats didn't.
Chloe, Ginger, Peter and Smokey
lay on her feet in turn to hold her
from walking away from life before
we were ready. One night, the cats knew
we'd never be ready, but she was.
They groomed themselves in the living room
as she crumpled in sweet relief. Now,
I hold each cat on my lap in turn,
the only poems I write some days.

Three hours to coax out the tap root
of an apple tree that's not thriving
and haul it with shovel and water
and a fruit tree fertilizer stake
and a delighted dog—*we're working!*
uphill to transplant near apple trees
my sister planted decades ago
in the clearing Mama and Daddy
intended for the house cancer stole
from them. This is my essay today.

A dexterous lifetime ago, he built
a cabin for me just far enough
into the woods to be out of sight
of all that needs tending on our farm
so I could attend to my thoughts. Now,
the stealthy airs of a war he thought
ended a salvaged lifetime ago
are breathing again in his neurons
as speculative fiction I might write
if I had the time and the heart.

I honor our farm's gardening ghosts
by tending their unfinished jobs,

beauty eases work. Mama planted
the cup-sized rose ones along the road.
The tiny pink bush was Lona Belle's,
one she missed digging up and moving
when she sold the farm, not the flowers,
to Mama and Daddy. I'm adding
deep coral native azaleas as
my chapter of a farm history
written in lines of flourishing blooms.

Unrelenting hard work is the thread.
Building, repairing, last-ditch patching,
tearing down. Clearing, planting, weeding,
giving over to chickweed, privet
and pine. Clearing again. Hauling glass, plastic,
balloons, diapers, downed trees and beer cans
to clear the creek until the next storm.
One generation rising strong as
new forest growth, then weakening
at the trunk, crumpling as their children
take up the connected narrative.
It's my story now, told most days
in work, not words.

And yet there is joy in the telling.
Who these days has their own woods to walk?
The dog and I head uphill to speak
to the young, and elderly apple trees,
praising them all for their endurance.
I lay my hands on their leaves. The dog waits,
knowing a prayer when he sees one.
Gratitude and petition tangle
like cat brier. I clear another stretch
of the path and my thoughts—my envoi
to whoever might be listening.

Pauletta Hansel

Genealogy

I come
from women / their history
erased   relentless
river   press
of time   stories
are stones   left
behind   a whisper
becomes history
                    sister / daughter
        mother /
cousin / aunt   a wild
entanglement
rough rock   /   drowned
        roots
a branch-strewn bank
my words call
        home

Pauletta Hansel

I'm Not in Your Town to Stay, Said a Lady Old and Gray
—(Etta Mullins Lewis, 1908-1993)

I can't hear that song without picturing
my granny, her hair roped up in its ashy bun,
a wad of tissue pulled from her cracked
vinyl purse, spilling quarters and dimes. *Yes,*
warden, I'm just here to get my baby out of jail.
Maybe Uncle Willie. His baby-round cheeks
and wispy hint of mustache. Or Ben, his
flint-eyed older brother. In the pen. Again.
Around my mother's maple table, all
the sisters sit. Coffee's percolating hum.
And I am…where? Invisible. Waiting as bright
coins of story fall through the cracks to me.
This time, a gun. The sisters shake their black
coifed heads and pat my granny's wrinkled hand.

"*Yes, warden, I'm just here to get my baby out of jail*" line from the song
by Karl Davis and Harty Taylor [Published 1934]

Pauletta Hansel

Self Portrait as the Old Woman Who Became a Goblin

This spinning thread of me
well satisfied
to rage and plague
whomever dares
to come by begging
what I will not give.
No.
Sew your want
inside your own
breast pocket.
I will dance myself
into a wizened wisp
of smoke,
delighted
above measure.

"The Old Woman Who Became A Goblin" Korean Folk Tales, Imps, Ghosts and Fairies by Im Bang & Yi Ryuk (Translated by James S. Gale) [Published 1913]

Kaja S. Parker

I Dream for Them

My mom is revoking our Christmas privileges again. We're in her bedroom. She's lying under a mound of comforters playing some farming game on her phone; I'm spinning around in the fuzzy white desk chair by the window. I stare out the window at the weathered duplexes and used cars. One of the cars is on its last leg, with remnants of a bumper dangling off the front of it. I know its owners don't have the money to get it fixed. None of us do. I look over to the TV. A poorly produced Hallmark movie is playing, *Christmas at Pemberley Manor*, a favorite of hers. I've been spending a lot of time talking to her on late nights like these during winter break. It's become our routine, and I love it so much I don't want to go back to college.

I ask her why there are no presents under the tree.

"Christmas is canceled," she says.

I'm not surprised. She's done this before. "Why?" I ask.

She shrugs. "Your siblings don't deserve it. They have terrible grades."
This is true. My siblings don't have a care in the world regarding their education. They complain, they bully, they procrastinate, they make trouble. I always wonder why I am so academically responsible and why that hasn't rubbed off on my siblings. I'm supposed to be their role model, and if you ask me, I am a damn good one. *So why am I the only one who attended the state's best high school?* I like to ask myself why they can't seem to succeed in school–*just work harder and apply yourself*–but deep down, I know why.

...

At seven, I was already a teacher's pet. In English, my favorite class, we started our day with creative writing prompts. I was so excited to continue the story I was working on: a fantasy story about a knight who journeys through a magical land and corresponds with his forbidden lover, documenting his adventures in his missives. Mildly mature content for a third-grader, right? I think I was destined to create complex characters and visceral, vivid stories.

Ms. Parker walked around our small, baby blue classroom, peering over students' shoulders. Pride in her alma mater was evident in everything she did: she filled the room with Berea College flags, sang songs about how "Berea can achieve" when we sat on the alphabet carpet for circle time, and proudly told us stories about her time as a college student. I remember loving our classroom; its decorations were colorful and homey. Because of my classroom's liveliness, I would've never considered CSR Academy a school for poor Black students in high-risk situations, but that's what it was. It was meant for my demographic–kids coming from impoverished homes, often living with single mothers and food stamps. It closed down a few years after I left due to underfunding. Typical.

Ms. Parker walked up behind me, her shirt a bright azure blue. "What are you writing, Kaja?" she asked me. Her auburn hair fell in her face. She was always curious about me. Looking back, if I didn't know any better, I would've been offended by the way this Southern white woman constantly seemed to investigate me. Is she going to ask to touch my hair? Ms. Parker wasn't like that, though. Those questions and speculations were for my own good.

I told her the gist of my story, of how instead of starting a new idea with a new prompt, I built upon my existing plot each day. While most of my classmates did the bare minimum for those prompts, I took them seriously. I was crafting a whole world in those fifteen minutes of writing. I think about that story often. I miss that world I'd created—it was the world that started them all. She was impressed by how detailed my story was. I smiled because external validation, especially in academic settings, has always been my greatest strength and weakness.

...

A few days later, rather than attending class like I usually would, I was told that I would be going to help my sister with her math work upstairs. It wasn't strange for me at the time: the year before, when my brother was in kindergarten, I would go to his class and read to the five-year-olds. I occasionally missed my classes to participate in the younger kids' classes. It wasn't weird then, but now, looking back, I realize how peculiar the situation was. There I was, a young third-grader, more concerned with who my "boyfriend" was or wasn't, going to other classrooms and missing my own classwork to help other kids with theirs.

Visiting other rooms was similar to being in Ms. Parker's English class. The teachers there inspected me, too. They were amazed that such a poor girl was as advanced as I was. Black girls from the hood weren't supposed to do anything but repeat generational curses—endure teen pregnancy, drop out of school, and so on. They didn't like school, and they definitely weren't going to college. But I did, and I was. Because I was the exception, I was under constant watch by every adult in that building. At that age, it didn't upset me. I liked the attention. Now, I loathe that I was subject to such gazes. I shouldn't be so peculiar. There should be more scholars who look like me. There could be more.

Even the custodians knew me: on my last day at CSR, one of them was walking by. I was in the hallway, heading to the principal's office, and he stopped and talked with me. I was friendly with the staff, but I wasn't a suck-up. I was just kind. However, to my peers, that automatically translated to "teacher's pet."

He said, "You're the smartest kid in this school."

I smiled and thanked him. *He's just being nice.*

"Seriously. You're gonna do big things one day."

I didn't know what to say, so I thanked him again.

He nodded and said, "Have a good summer."

That was the last time I ever saw him, but I remember that interaction as if it happened yesterday. During that brief encounter, I felt seen. There was nothing I prided myself on more than being intelligent, and I was glad someone I hardly knew could recognize that. But I also felt pressured, like I had to be the smartest person in every room for the rest of my life. Like I had to prove my worth to everyone.

Once I was in Mrs. Morgernstern's office, I sat across from her at her desk. She smiled at me.

"How's your last day of third grade going?" she asked.

"It's fun! We're going to the park soon." That park was the location of many a shooting, but we had fun running around on the graffitied pavement.

"That sounds awesome! Well, I wanted to give you something." She reached beneath her desk and pulled out a box set of books. There were three of them, each a pretty pastel color. *The Sisterhood of the Traveling Pants.* I tried not to cry as I read the backs of them. It wasn't so much the books themselves, but the principle behind receiving them. The books weren't all that mind-blowing, but they were mine. I didn't have many books growing up because they're not cheap and are easily perishable. That gift changed my life; it was the first series I'd ever read. And to think they came from the principal, not a teacher that'd I'd spent hours in class with, was even more profound. This woman, who didn't know me from a can of paint, opened the floodgates I didn't realize were there. It was like a dam had been destroyed, and pouring out like a waterfall was my love for literature. I just wanted more books and more words. Years later, and I *still* want more. There will never be enough sentences to satiate me.

She said, "I will be in contact with you and your family when you're at Hyde Park. If there's ever anything you need, don't hesitate to reach out."

She wasn't lying. Over the years, she's done so much for me. She would buy me school supplies. She would buy me books. She would write letters of recommendation. She came to my graduation. She took me to the movies and for ice cream on my birthdays, which I had rarely done before. Mrs. Morgenstern constantly went out of her way to support me, though I didn't realize how significant it was back then.

...

It was years later when Ms. Parker told me the story of how she completely altered the course of my life. We were having dinner a few months after I graduated high school. Her quaint apartment smelled of tomatoes and Italian seasoning. Quiet pop music played from her speaker, and outside the sky was darkening. The view from her window was breathtaking: the silhouette of the city and the lush greenery surrounding it looked more like a painting than real life. The sunset was clear, not a dim streetlight blocking it. It was a welcome change from the dejected neighborhood where I lived. Even the air smelled different. It smelled clean, like it had just been washed, dried, and folded. On my side of town, it smelled like waste and gasoline. *You'll be living this comfortably one day,* I told myself.

We reminisced about the past, our CSR days, how I was a meager child then, and how I'd grown into the young adult sipping water at her counter.

"You were always so dedicated. I remember thinking, wow, I have never met a child like this before," she said.

I smiled, thinking about how savvy I was back then. It felt good knowing that even after my mediocrity in high school, I was competent at some point. Going to acclaimed schools really makes you feel insignificant: it's no longer an impressive feat to have high test scores; everyone does.

"I just knew you were bigger than that school. You passed everything with flying colors. You were too smart for your own good, so I spoke to the chair and told him that you needed to be tested."

Tested, in this case, meant that she wanted me to take the test for the Cincinnati Gifted Academy program to see how I performed.

"So, he had us evaluate you in class, and once he saw for himself, we got you scheduled."

Scheduled the entrance and IQ tests I took one day during my third-grade year. It was the test that transferred me from CSR Academy, a school for poor Black people, to Hyde Park School, a school for well-off white people.

I was the only Black girl in my grade. I wasn't used to being around so many white people at once; I was used to predominantly Black—and, apparently, hood—communities. I wasn't used to Latin classes and packed lunches; I was used to BrainPop Jr. and government-funded lunches. My classmates wondered how I grew out my hair when I wore box braids. I wondered how they had so many exciting clothes because we wore boring khaki uniforms at CSR. It was all so new and overwhelming.

There were so many times I felt I didn't belong there. I felt I had been misled. That old custodian, all those teachers, my family: everyone expected greatness from me. I was going to change the world and the narrative. But I was no longer the exception. I was just like everyone else. Going to Hyde Park and Walnut Hills destroyed all the dignity I had. I thought I was no longer special. *Who am I if not the smartest person in the room? What am I good for?*

I still understood language better than most ten-year-olds. On Fun Fridays, I always finished the word searches first. I could read at the collegiate level. I created stories and intricate scenes in my head. If nothing else, the bibliophile in me flourished at Hyde Park. We had access to so many books, and I probably read every one of them.

"I knew you were brilliant," Ms. Parker said.

I know it now, too. I might not be Einstein, but at least I have my passion. My *purpose*. I've been lucky enough to dream at dusk and have them come true at dawn. I'm brilliant and blessed. So many curious Black minds would do anything to learn, read, create, and imagine. But my reality is not shared by a good number of them. The ability to read and write and fantasize is a gift I'll want under my Christmas tree forever. It's taken me until now to realize my poeticism is my power. My pens are magical because I'm the one writing with them.

In this oppressive world, I was never meant to write. I was never meant to understand the potential of language. A wise person once said, "Words are freedom." I was meant to stay trapped in a small cell, never to experience that freedom. Reading and writing have taken me farther than I've ever traveled before. They've taken me to Prythian and Gavaldon. They've brought me to tears and laughter. They've allowed me to be what I didn't think I could be: an innovator and a visionary. And had it not been for Ms. Parker and Mrs. Morgenstern, I'm not sure I would've escaped that prison.

So, yes, I will be a teacher's pet until my last breath. I will be the only one reading a novel in a room full of nomophobes. I will ramble about the random story ideas I'll probably never write. Why? Because I was fortunate enough to have support in a system built against me. Because my ancestors knew the possibilities that literacy unlocks. They fought for the education I have. Now, I fight for them. I write for them. I read for them. I dream for them.

Kari Gunter-Seymour

You Must be Born Again

I gave up religion long ago
thanks to my speak-in-tongues mother,
all tendon and teeth, jabbing me

with sermons, her silhouette
slipping every door,
tumbling me ass over ashes.

I swore I'd gussy up, brave city life
when I came of age, the heat
of my heartbeats goosebumping
a surly furbish to my skin.

Mama would laugh herself blue-faced,
clap my cheeks red,
her mouth a howl and blizzard,

her sass a scat of alley cats,
all tits and elbows,
a growling clash of bite and scratch.

Even dismay can zing
when aligned with comeuppance.
When I left, I left in the night,
my wings torn from her back.

Kari Gunter-Seymour

Where I Come From

A deluge of droplets
after months of scalding sun,
the little that's left of us stomping
two-by-two through swollen waters.

Oh the corporate histories
written here, eulogized
in ruin and rust, a land plucked
and pimped, targets stapled
to our hillbilly backs.

Drylanders, smug, clueless
shake confused heads, ask
why don't you move?

Here our measuring cups
are Holy Writ, our covenants
carried on tongues, roots
pleached, washed in the blood,
a chemistry of all who dwelt before us.

Here even toddlers know
the alchemy of survival,
how to spit-chew a jewelweed poultice
to sooth a bite or sting,
yarrow fronds to calm a scraped knee.

A gang of crows chase a hawk,
insects I will never learn all the names of
skate the surface of this drowned ground
thinking they can trust the journey.

A kingfisher swoops in like King Coal,
swallows up all he possibly can,
swaggers his fat belly skyward.

Kari Gunter-Seymour

This Week, the Drought

On this land where creek beds
splinter and crack,
squirrels are skeletons lugging fur,
the deer pale as papery birch.
Hornets hover, plummet,
bounce off hard ground,
birds kilter like ashes.

I walk out into another scalding dawn
where, overnight, a mast of acorns,
freed from shriveled stalks,
scattered themselves like mana
far as my eye can see.
Squirrel and deer stand side-by-side,
heads bowed, relishing.
Birds balance branches, salivate
the chance of leftover crumbs.
A watering bucket in hand,
I suffer myself to hope.

Sherrell Runnion Wigal

Last Duty

> *—And there shall be a great cry throughout all the land… –Exod. 11:6 KJV*

For days we wailed and wept,
knowing there was no Lazarus
among us. Our bodies, heavy
as wet clay. Unrested
we gathered unto ourselves,
came to this last duty of death.

And after the mourners,
the pale words of comfort,
the long cortege, we left
not now knowing hunger,
the chores of daily living,
we had forgotten
even our own names.

Sherrell Runnion Wigal

Upon Us
—I will bring you up out of the affliction…" –Exod. 3:17 KJV)

It was October and we gathered,
our hearts so far apart,
yet tenderness was upon us.

The hum of the moment
heavy inside our ears,
we held our arms—both close and wide,
holding ourselves and each other
while, in the fragility of dusk and dark,
time closed upon us.

The following hours unbidden,
thick our throats and tongues, empty
our hands, shallow the days ahead,
unleaven upon us.

Karen Spears Zacharias

A Little More Time

Lindy made her grandmother promise that before heading out to Hake's grave that Tuesday morning, she would stop by Albright's Florist and pick up the arrangement Lindy had ordered over the Internet. Mamie had no idea how somebody way out in Ory-gun could place an order for flowers in Georgia over the Internet. Still, she swore to the Barefooted Jesus and all the Saints in New Orleans that she wouldn't dare go out to Hake's grave without picking up the flowers Lindy ordered.

"Make sure there are no carnations in the mix," Lindy said. "I hate carnations. I told Mrs. Albright to use sunflowers. Daddy always liked sunflowers."

"Yes," Mamie said. "I remember." Hake hadn't been but six years old when the two of them planted sunflowers around his sandbox in the backyard. Mamie had read in *Southern Living* that if planted in a pattern, sunflowers would grow to form their very own fort. With his little hands gripping a garden trowel, Hake shoveled out a trench on the outside of the sandbox's 2x4s while Mamie followed along behind him, scooping aside dirt with her gloved hand, and sprinkling in the seeds. She gave Hake a handful of seeds to plant as well.

The very next morning, she'd found Hake sitting on the back stoop, his fuzzy blankey wrapped around his shoulders.

"What are you doing out here?" Mamie asked. "It's not even 7 a.m.!"

"I'm waiting on the sunflowers," Hake replied.

"Oh, honey, those aren't going to grow for a very long time."

"But in the book the plants grow up overnight!" he protested.

"What book?" Mamie sat on the stoop beside her boy and pulled him onto her lap.

"Jack and the Beanstalk," he replied.

Mamie pressed her cheek into Hake's gold curls. "Oh, yes, that book. Well, you see, books have more magic than our world. In books, seeds grow overnight. In this world, they take a little more time than that."

Hake took his mother's face between his tiny palms and stared deep into her brown eyes: "Let's move there, then."

"Where?" Mamie asked. She often had a difficult time keeping up with Hake's way of thinking. She wasn't sure if it was because he was a boy, or if it was because he was a child. "Where is it you want to go live?"

"In the book world!" Hake replied, his tone full of five-year-old indignation. "The land of magic!"

"I'm afraid that's not possible, son."

"Why not? Gumby and Pokey do it."

"Gumby and Pokey aren't human like us," Mamie said. The May sun had risen over the tree line and was warming them both. "How about pancakes for breakfast, would you like that?"

Hake jumped up and ran barefoot into the kitchen. "Yummm. Pancakes are my favorite!"

Hake waited all summer long for those seeds to grow. After his daily nap, he would fill his Superman thermos and water all the way around his sandbox. When he spotted the first shoot breaking through, he jumped up and down, waving his arms as if trying to take flight, and hollering for Mamie to "Come See, Mama! Come See!". By the time the maples started yellowing and the temperatures had dropped to a coolish 70s of autumn, instead of the usual high 90s of summer, the seeds had indeed done as the article in Southern Living promised, formed a fort of sunflowers. Mamie took a photo of little Hake standing between the towering stalks with the bright yellow heads, his grin as broad as the brim on the baseball cap he wore. It was her favorite snapshot of her boy, the one that always reminded her of Hake's exuberance for all things living.

No mother expects to outlive her child, and given that Hake was her only child, Mamie dealt with a crushing waterfall of sorrow. A force that flattened her, left her gasping for breath, and the feeling that she was never, ever going to be able to escape from the darkness again. Well-meaning friends, who at first had been so loving about her loss, had grown weary of seeking to comfort her over the years. Many stopped calling, stopped inviting her out to lunch or to book club. It surprised Mamie how many dear friends had simply given up on her. Even her own mother chided Mamie during their weekly phone call.

"I really don't think you are handling this all that well," Mrs. Bickerstaff said. "It's been five years, Mamie. Hake wouldn't want you to…"

"Mother, please don't," Mamie interrupted. She hated being rude to her mother, but she no longer had the ability, or the will, to tolerate others telling her how she ought to get over Hake's death. She quickly changed the subject. "How's the new pastor working out?"

"He's a lovely man," Mrs. Bickerstaff replied. "Younger than Zell but not as young as Lindy. But, of course, the old timers at St. James's don't much care for him. They are so set in their ways."

Mamie chuckled. Mrs. Bickerstaff would turn 100 in December. She and Lindy had been planning a surprise celebration for months now. But she did have to hand it to her mother, Mrs. Bickerstaff was admired throughout Baldwin County for her fierce independence, brilliant mind, and undeterred progressiveness. Mrs. Bickerstaff didn't retire from her job as the library's Learning and Development Director until her 88th birthday, and only then because she said she had other adventures to pursue. At 91, she published her first book—*Secret Sisters: The Cloistered Nuns of Madrid*—to critical acclaim, even landing on the front page of Al.com and garnering a favorable review in the *New York Times Book Review*. She was in better health than many people half her age, something she rarely failed to mention whenever any remarked about her age.

"Stubbornness is a trait we all battle, I guess," Mamie said.

"Some of us more than others," Mrs. Bickerstaff replied. The observation wasn't lost on Mamie. She knew her mother meant it more as commentary on her, than on the congregants of St. James.

"You never lost a child, Momma. You don't know how difficult it is."

"Hake was no child. He was 58."

"He was still my son. I will forever and always consider him my child."

The two women slipped into a crevasse of icy silence.

"I've got to go, Momma," Mamie finally said.

"You going out to the gravesite?" Mrs. Bickerstaff knew the answer before she even asked it.

"It's the 5th anniversary," Mamie said, wondering if perhaps her mother had forgotten.

"Yes, I remember," she replied. But she also knew that even if it hadn't been the anniversary of Hake's death, Mamie would still be going out to the grave, like she had most every day since Hake had given up the ghost. She understood what Mamie had not yet figured out—that she was going there not for Hake's benefit but for her own. Mamie simply could not forgive herself for all the ways she figured she had failed her son.

"I promised Lindy I would take some flowers over to her daddy's grave."

"Is Zell going with you?"

"I don't know. I haven't asked her," Mamie replied.

"Don't you think you should?"

"I don't know why," Mamie replied. "She ain't been out to the grave but once or twice since Hake died. Pearl is always making excuses for her, but the truth is she helped put him the ground."

"Now, Mamie, you don't know that." Mrs. Bickerstaff was exasperated with her daughter.

"Like hell I don't. I really have to go, Momma. Bye."

Mrs. Bickerstaff heard the phone click before she could utter a half-decent "Goodbye". Opening the fridge door, she reached for a Kombucha, twisted off the top and poured the amber nectar into one of her best crystal goblets.

Mrs. Bickerstaff believed in using only her best china and glassware even on a regular old Tuesday. She figured anyone who had lived as long as she had earned whatever daily indulgences one could muster. Some drank a Bud Lite from an aluminum can. Others preferred a glass of Pinot Grigio. Mrs. Bickerstaff had been drinking the fermented tea known for its medicinal properties since she was first introduced to it on a trip to China in the 1990s. It was her go-to drink, and she believed wholeheartedly the elixir had helped her outlive her own grandson. She had tried her darndest to get Hake to drink it, but he protested: "I might as well drink a jar of water fished from a dirty toilet as to drink that nasty smelling stuff!"

Hake was every bit as stubborn as his momma. "A person's weakness is just their strength cranked up a notch too high," Mrs. Bickerstaff proclaimed to the cardinals flitting about on the birdhouses on the porch. She didn't really expect that Hake could hear her, but she raised her glass to her deceased grandson anyway. "You did us all proud, son. Well, except for marrying Zell but none of that matters now, does it?" Mrs. Bickerstaff laughed and tipped her glass back. "Lord God that tastes like dirt!" she declared but took another gulp anyway. Given her age, Mrs. Bickerstaff figured she would be swallowing dirt one way or another.

Sherry Cook Stanforth

Wash Away My Home (Song)

There's a hole in the heart of Kentucky
Where the mountains once rose up to the sun
Now the rain is falling down over barren torn ground
Wash away, wash away my home

I grew up in Harlan Country running through the wild woods
Skipping rocks in singing mountains streams
When the cloak of evening fell we would watch the ghostly fog
Winding up the mountain like a dream

Once I gained a couple years my grandma took me by the hand
And led me to a graveyard on the hill
Though I never knew those people, they became a part of me
Now the graves lie under mounds of till

There's a hole in the heart of Kentucky
Where the mountains once rose up to the sun
Now the rain is falling down over barren torn ground
Wash away, wash away my home

When I left out on my own I took my knowledge from my home
Healing plants and songs to fill the day
I went back to bury Daddy, in another year my mom
But I lost them when that mountain fell away

I know miles and miles of bends—I've had some trees that I call friends
I've been baptized by the sun upon the ridge
When I see that coal-black slag choking out the living land
I face a gap impossible to bridge

There's a hole in the heart of Kentucky
Where the mountains once rose up to the sun
Now the rain is falling down over barren torn ground
Wash away, wash away my home

If our past comes back to haunt us, I've been haunted by my land
In the shadows where I rest, I sometimes pray
That my children's children know, we take nothing when we go
But the love of home and dust from better days

There's a hole in the heart of Kentucky
Where the mountains once rose up to the sun
Now the rain is falling down over barren torn ground
Wash away, wash away my home

Omope Carter Daboiku

Old-Fashioned

Breakfast for dinner; dinner for breakfast.
Fried okra with eggs, or succotash of okra, corn, tomatoes with fish.
Liver and onions, with gravy over rice.
Pizza came compliments of Chef Boyardee; a grill-smoked burger
      was in your own backyard.
Daddy said, "It's time to head across the mountains," where we took long walks amid
      no see-ums to the spring where newts declared the water pure and drinkable.
Buckets on either end of a pole held across my shoulders—
      a pioneer throw-back from the future.
Milking cows, churning butter and running to meet my (great) Uncle Jimmy
      coming home, covered in lime, looking as white as he was not.
Will we stop at the General Store along the road?
Will there be a nickel for Nehi?—colder and tastier against
      the red clay heat of Appomattox.
No electricity, no running water don't phase me none,
      cause there's plenty of love and fine food straight from the Earth.
Squash and eggs, fried corn, wild game shot with bow and arrow.
Pickles, dill and sweet, from last summer's cukes
      waiting to go crunch in our mouths.
We chop wood with abandon, having fun playing with sharp blades.
Elders sit and watch from afar as we do the work putting wood in the pile,
      for short winter days and long winter nights,
      being careful of snakes hiding within.
The stove and the fireplaces both need to be fed; and,
I can start a one match-fire in a pouring rain, should I ever need to.

Omope Carter Daboiku

Blood Legacy and Laundry

I am the blood of Aganju
flowing from inside my mother, claiming this land of my birth.
I am the foam on Yemonja's breast as I suckle the word
and am nourished by saltwater wisdom.
I am the hidden and escape the Trail so that my eyes remain dry
        when hidden heritage is brought to light.
I am mist to the mothers of my youth, who in their toiling sang
        sensual intonations of struggle so that their husband, "Jesus",
        might sooth their sorrow.
Entrepreneurs—the sweat of their brow created by the ingenuity
        of their own brains—the steam, the starch,
        the baskets of other folks' luxury.
I remember tellin my momma, "If it ain't drip dry, I ain't wearin it."
        declaring my freedom from the iron—flat or electric.
Then, spent 15 years in traditional Yoruba clothes,
        walking around carrying the past on my back.
Child of Cotton,
Red Earth Child.

Jonie McIntire

To the tiny, twitchy woman

who sat in the back corner
at the basement barroom
late-spring poetry reading,
just after the memo was leaked
about Roe versus Wade being
overturned and I was so angry
that I said *I didn't even want
to talk about it,* but I did anyway
and the crowd was quiet and I
couldn't tell if that was distance
or indifference, and I read
my angry poem and my abortion
poem and I said a lot of my poems
are *just for the ladies,* but nobody
laughed, and I felt that quiet crush
of awkward and wrong,
but you walked up afterward
and you were gushing about how you
needed to hear that and you understood
everything I said and it's exhausting
we still have to fight like this but, hell,
here we are, and as you left with my
little book and a flyer, I remembered
how brave can feel small but grows
and it made me hungry.

Jonie McIntire

New Listing - Zestimate $255,000

What we see on the third or fourth frame
is the skin wall, the seafoam green sheen
over our childhood. A fisheye shot
of the newly renovated kitchen makes a landscape
made of dreams and perspective,

far different than grandma's steaming
pot of potatoes setting atop
summer-camp woven potholder
as she, bright red-fingered peeled
and cut into a wide yellow plastic
bowl, the trick to her famous

potato salad—a mix of burned fingers,
cheap mustard, onions diced in her hands
(never on a cutting board) and real mayonnaise,
the kind that goes as translucent as
powdered potatoes when left uneaten.

She would have laughed at these pictures
of kitchen and basement. How in fifty years
they never looked like this, even when
there were 5 kids toiling to make it look so.
She earned her layer of grease, her water
stains, her oh so dusty corners.

Two bathrooms, four bedrooms.
One thousand, six hundred and ninety-two
square feet. With a tree missing in back
where one son hung himself. A spot
in the front yard where the apple tree
grew that a girl fighting off hungry hands
climbed for top branches to wait and hide.

No trace of the holes in drywall from
skulls smacked, the remnants of doors
with locks shattered under persistent weight,
their hollow innards revealed through
fist-shaped windows. No echoes of the sound
of boxed ears or repetitious slapping.

North Allegheny School district. Close to Ross Park Mall
and emergency rooms that will remember. This
is where we lived and grew. Where she died.
Listed by Howard Hanna. Sold 10/25/22.

E.J. Wade

It's Not Like It Used to Be

Their knees are not as strong
as they used to be.

Chafed and calloused
by wood and tile,
they tell the story of
lye and wax, twice a day
and sometimes in between
sullied by the remnants of mudded boot
and sacred paws.
There is no consideration given
to age or constitution.

Their hands are not as steady
as they used to be.

Scarred and hardened
by oven and iron,
they tell the story of
yeast and starch
rising before the sun comes up
pressing down, long after the sun sets.
There is no consideration given
to age or constitution.

Their feet are not as sturdy
as they used to be.

Tired and worn,
they tell the story of
bondage and protest
placing one foot before the other
slipping and sliding
one step at a time.

There is no consideration given
for age or constitution.

Their backs are not as straight
as they used to be.

Bent, bruised, and broken
they tell the story of
backlash against backside
backs kissed by the sun
and repressed by iron
they acquiesce, laying down their burden.
There is no consideration given
for age or constitution.

E.J. Wade

Goldenrod

Sister put a mirror in front of her face
and she didn't like what she saw
so, she took baby girl's finger paints
and colored her hair goldenrod

she outlined her eyes to match those
of the Egyptian queen on the post card
her friend sent her while on vacation

tracing the shape of her mouth
she drew a thin red line within the
contour of her lips camouflaging
the royal thickness bequeathed by her ancestors

with the skill of a painter
she sketched and fashioned
a nose keen and narrow
the kind that Greek sculptors adored

turning her head from side-to-side
she smiled at the face in the mirror
pleased with what she had created

breaking open the pretty pink piggybank
she gathered the loose change
and stacked the copper pennies,
along the windowsill

tallying the coins over and over
until her eyes watered
she gathered them up as an offering
to the man with the antique Polaroid

Sister put a mirror in front of her face
and wetted her lips
before smiling for the camera

Tess Lloyd

Cedar Apples

1.

To grow old is to dwell in a creaking kingdom the young mostly cannot know. The young have not echoed once through Tara's halls, nor lain in bed full of memory and despair, listening for the old body electric's new chant, the esoterica of the mage, who is years, who is pear blossoms scattered across wet grass and bent fingers that no longer revel in the flow of ink from the harp-like pen onto the page to echo the budded silver apples that frost will shrivel, though someday the young will see that they too have been duped by the mage, as irresistibly as rain bludgeoning pear blossoms, grass swallowing petals greenly, blindly, like her husband, and this is why she hates her son, who when he walks up from the orchard looks so much like his father that her chest aches, but always it is her son coming up from the orchard with his dark hair flying, her son on whose shoulders pear blossoms are falling, her son whom she hates purely and loves purely because he is alive, and although she would with her life shield him from the sullen realm into which the mage shoves hopeful aspirants, it is her son striding up from the orchard through the grass, soaking his cuffs in the dew, while her husband has wandered past the blind grass, past the pear dust, past the chant and the echo, to gather cedar apples, and without looking back over his shoulder stepped down the river bank into the waiting ferry.

2.

beyond pear dust
beyond cedar apples
beyond petals staining green grass blindly
beyond her husband stepping down the bank into the waiting ferry

Tess Lloyd

Give Thanks for Sagging Barbed Wire: 1945

When the ride you hitched in Spruce Pine drops you at the lane to your father's farm, you see what three years at the front made you forget: barbed wire sagging between canted fence posts, ash leaves shaking like starlings, weeds the truck tires don't erase from the middle of the dirt lane pointing to the house that is invisible from here except for the attic gable where at fourteen you moved your bed to get away from your kid brother even though sleeping beneath the metal roof was hotter than inside that tank at Oran in '42. But forgetting, like remembering, is immaterial, and so you adjust your garrison cap and walk along the weedy strip through dew that soaks your dress khakis to the knees, not that it matters now, and rounding the hill where your father pastured bull calves that when they escaped trampled the tobacco and mules that swished their scrawny tails against the flies, you come upon the house, gray weatherboard and the yard still smelling of the fatback your mother fried for breakfast this morning, your mother who now waits on the porch with her hands folded across her stomach, her smile fading into the usual resignation as you drop your duffle bag in the dirt and keep walking, walking, past the barn where your father is tinkering with another tobacco-setting contraption, along the edge of the field where your brother is plowing a red clay field so steep a tractor will flip before you know it, like with Old Man Bolejack on the North Toe, whom they didn't find for hours, although pinned beneath three tons of metal it's always too late, like that damned deathtrap at Anzio, but you do not call *Remember Anzio, remember Old Man Bolejack,* lest you remind gravity to grow greedy, instead you walk on, through the hayfield your father never limed and so he baled broomsedge, across the saddle where you walloped your brother with a hickory limb for something you don't remember and he never snitched, until on the far side of Baldy you reach the cedars you helped your father set out when he bought the farm because he planned to cut fence posts someday and never did, and where today you lean against a ragged trunk, light a Lucky, give thanks for sagging barbed wire, the smell of cedar, buzzards soaring over Ripshin Ridge.

Contributor Notes

April J. Asbury is a writer, teacher, and editor from southwest Virginia. She earned her M.F.A. from Spalding University and M.A. from Hollins. Her work appears in *Artemis, Still: The Journal, The Anthology of Appalachian Writers*, and other publications. Finishing Line Press published her first poetry collection, *Woman with Crows*.

KB Ballentine teaches creative writing, theatre arts, and literature to high school and college students, her home nestled at the base of the Appalachian Mountains in Tennessee. Ballentine's eighth collection *Spirit of Wild* was published by Blue Light Press in March 2023. Find out more at www.kbballentine.com.

Jennifer Browne falls in love easily with other people's dogs. She is the author of *American Crow* (Beltway Editions, 2024) and the poetry chapbooks *whisper song* (tiny wren publishing, 2023) and *The Salt of the Geologic World* (Bottlecap Press, 2023). She lives in Frostburg, Maryland. https://linktr.ee/jenniferabrowne

Sarah Diamond Burroway is an eastern Kentucky native whose writing has been published by *Still: The Journal, The Bitter Southerner, Women Speak, In Parentheses*, and others. She works as a nonprofit grants person and earned her MFA in Nonfiction from Eastern Kentucky University's Bluegrass Writers Studio.

Devin Aeh Canary is a queer homeschooling mama and cofounder of Canary Acres Animal Sanctuary. Devin is a wannabe witch who believes that words, spoken or written, can be magic spells that alter someone's existence, for just a minute or for much longer. She believes poetry is powerful—poetry is witchcraft.

Catherine Carter's collections of poetry with LSU Press include *The Memory of Gills, The Swamp Monster at Home*, and *Larvae of the Nearest Stars*. She is a professor of English at Western Carolina University in the Great Smoky Mountains.

Sheila Carter-Jones is the author of *Every Hard Sweetness, Three Birds Deep*, which won the Naomi Long Madgett Poetry Book Award, and her chapbook *Crooked Star Dream Book* was named Honorable Mention for the New York Center for Book Arts Chapbook Contest. She was born and raised in a small coal mining town in Western Pennsylvania which is the site for many of her poems. sheilo512@aol.com

Odana Chaney is from Culloden, WV. As the 2024 New River Gorge Creative in Residence at Lafayette Flats, she has appeared in *Women Speak, About Place Journal*, and elsewhere. She attended the University of Pittsburgh where she found her voice but forgot to graduate. She writes about dirt, duality, and dearness.

Sheree Stewart Combs resides with her husband on a farm in central Kentucky. She grew up in Letcher County Kentucky, deep in the Appalachians, and travels 'home' as often as possible. Sheree's publication history includes essays in *Heartwood Literary Magazine* and *Beyond Words International Magazine of Literature and Art*.

Beth Copeland is the author of *Shibori Blue: Thirty-six Views of The Peak* (Redhawk Publications, 2024): *Selfie with Cherry* (Glass Lyre Press, 2022); *Blue Honey*, 2017 Dogfish Head Poetry Prize winner; *Transcendental Telemarketer* (BlazeVOX, 2012); and *Traveling through Glass*, 1999 Bright Hill Press Poetry Book Award winner.

Jessica Cory is the Editor of *Appalachian Journal: A Regional Studies Review*, published since 1972 at Appalachian State University. She's the editor of *Mountains Piled upon Mountains: Appalachian Nature Writing in the Anthropocene* (WVU Press, 2019) and the co-editor of *Appalachian Ecocriticism and the Paradox of Place* (UGA Press, 2023).

Danielle Kelly Curry grew up in Beverly, WV and now resides in Indiana with her husband. Currently, she serves as Assistant Teaching Professor of English at Ball State University. A two-time pushcart prize nominee, her work has appeared in *rkvry, Hedge Apple Magazine,* and *Women Speak* (vol. 5 & 7).

Designated a master teaching artist in 1990 by the Ohio Arts Council, **Omope Carter Daboiku** has performed across the US and on four continents. An award-winning community producer for WYSO's (91.3FM) West Dayton Stories, her storytelling is archived on YouTube, Ohio Arts Council's website, and Dayton Metro Library.

A retired WV public television producer, **Mary Lucille DeBerry** has had poems published in *Anthology of Appalachian Writers, Appalachian Heritage, Appalachian Journal, Heartwood,* and *Voices from the Attic.* She has three published collections: *Bertha Butcher's Coat* (2009) (Revised 2020); *Alice Saw the Beauty* (2014); and *She Was the Girl* (2020)

Morgan DePue is a neurodivergent Southern Appalachian poet with deep West Virginia roots. She lives in Ashe County, North Carolina, and teaches at Appalachian State University. Her work has appeared in various literary journals including *Bloodshot Journal of Contemporary Poetry, Main Street Rag Magazine,* and *Wild Goose Poetry Review.*

Danita Dodson is an educator, literary scholar, and the author of three poetry collections: *Trailing the Azimuth, The Medicine Woods,* and Between Gone and Everlasting. Her poems have appeared in *Salvation South* and elsewhere. She was born, and still resides, in Sneedville (Hancock County), Tennessee. Read more at www.danitadodson.com.

Mitzi Dorton has work in *Rattle/Appalachian Poets, SEMO Press, Poetry South, The Orchards Journal, Southern Literary Review Shadowplay, Otherwise Engaged,* and others. Her writing is forthcoming in Apofenie, Ukraine. She is author of the book, *Chief Corn Tassel* (Finishing Line Press), a Literary Global Book Award finalist in history and biography.

Award-winning poet, essayist, and teacher, **Kathleen Driskell** is the author of six books of poetry including *Goat-Footed Gods,* from Carnegie-Mellon University Press. Her poems and essays have appeared in *The New Yorker, River Teeth, Appalachian Review, Shenandoah, Southern Review,* and *Rattle.* Kathleen is Chair of the Naslund-Mann Graduate School of Writing at Spalding University.

Monic Ductan teaches at Tennessee Tech University. Her story collection, *Daughters of Muscadine,* won the Weatherford Award from Berea College. Monic's writing has appeared in a number of journals, including *Oxford American, Appalachian Review, Still,* and *Shenandoah.*

A native East Tennessean, **Sue Weaver Dunlap** lives deep in the Southern Appalachian Mountains near Walland, Tennessee. Her work has appeared in various journals. Her poetry books include *A Walk to the Spring House* (Iris Press, 2021), *Knead* (Main Street Rag, 2016), and *The Story Tender* (Finishing Line Press, 2014).

Christina Fisanick is President of the Writers Association of Northern Appalachia (WANA) and co-host of WANA LIVE!. She teaches writing at Pennsylvania Western University. In addition, she is the editor or author of more than thirty books. Her upcoming books: *Pulling the Thread: Untangling Wheeling History* (North Meridian 2024) and *"We Are Here!": New Writing from Northern Appalachia* (University of Kentucky 2025).

Lynette Ford is a fourth-generation, Black Appalachian storyteller and writer, and an Ohio teaching artist. The old neighborhoods of her childhood no longer exist, but their memories, and the wooded hills, river valleys, steel mills, railways and people that defined them remain touchpoints in her life and work.

Dreama Wyant Frisk, a native of McCann's Run, near Westin, West Virginia, now lives in Arlington, Virginia, but cherishes her roots and maintains her connections to loved ones in the Mountain State.

Connie Jordan Green lives on a hilltop farm in East Tennessee where she writes poetry, novels for young people, and, for over 42 years, a newspaper column. Her work has received numerous awards, including Pushcart nominations for the poetry. Although retired from full-time teaching, she frequently leads writing workshops.

Kari Gunter-Seymour is the Poet Laureate of Ohio, the editor of eleven anthologies, author of three collections of poetry and the winner of a POTY Award, Storytrade Award, Legacy Award and Best Book Award. Her work has been featured in *The New York Times, Poem-a-Day, American Book Review* and *World Literature Today*. Find her at www.kariguterseymourpoet.com.

Pauletta Hansel's ten poetry collections include *Will There Also Be Singing?* (Shadelandhouse Modern Press, 2024) poems of witness about Hansel's native Appalachia and this nation; *Heartbreak Tree* (Madville Publications, 2022), which won the Poetry Society of Virginia's 2023 North American Book Award; and Weatherford Award winner, *Palindrome*.

Melissa Helton is Literary Arts Director of Hindman Settlement School in southeastern Kentucky. Her work has appeared in *Shenandoah, Still: The Journal, Anthology of Appalachian Writers*, and more. Her chapbooks include *Inertia: A Study*, and *Hewn*. She is a dual citizen in the United Kingdom.

Sara Henning is the author of the poetry collections *Burn* (Southern Illinois University Press, 2024), *Terra Incognita* (Ohio University Press, 2022), and *View from True North* (Southern Illinois University Press, 2018). She's an assistant professor of creative writing at Marshall University, where she coordinates the A.E. Stringer Visiting Writers Series.

A native of upper East Tennessee, **Jane Hicks** is an award-winning poet, teacher, and quilter. Her poetry appears in both journals and numerous anthologies, including *Southern Poetry Anthology: Contemporary Appalachia* and *Southern Poetry Anthology: Tennessee*. Her newest book, *The Safety of Small Things* debuted in January of 2024 from the University Press of Kentucky under the Hearthside imprint.

Meredith S. Jensen is a writer, artist, and performer living in Athens County, OH. For employment, she develops museum exhibits; for enjoyment, she birds, hikes, gardens, reads, practices henna art, and makes lists. She resides in a hollow with her partner, orange cat, umbrella cockatoo, and occasionally two collegiate gremlins.

Jennifer Schomburg Kanke's work has appeared in *New Ohio Review, Massachusetts Review, Shenandoah* and *Salamander*. Her collection about Scioto County, Ohio, *The Swellest Wife Anyone Ever Had*, was published in the fall of 2024. She can be found on YouTube as *Meter&Mayhem*, a channel focusing on interviews with contemporary writers.

Nicole Karch is a poet and professional writer in Zanesville, Ohio. Her love for Appalachia began during her studies at Cornell University, where she (rather recklessly) explored numerous foothills and waterfalls. She is currently writing a collection of poems that explores Northern Appalachian identity and her ancestral ties to the region.

Leatha Kendrick, poet and teacher, grew up in Kentucky's Pennyroyal region, raised a family in the Appalachians, and lives in Lexington's verdant Bluegrass. Her writing appears in anthologies including *Women Speak; The Southern Poetry Anthology, Volume 3*; and *What Comes Down to Us – Twenty-Five Contemporary Kentucky Poets*.

Stephanie Kendrick is the 2023/25 Athens, Ohio Poet Laureate. She is the author of In *Any of These Towns* (Sheila-Na-Gig editions, 2022) and is the editor of local poetry newsletter, *Periodical Poetry*. With a master's in social sciences from Ohio University, she serves her local community in a variety of ways.

Patsy Kisner is the author of two books of poetry, *Last Days of an Old Dog* and *Inside the Horse's Eye*, both from Finishing Line Press. Her poetry has appeared in *Untelling, Still: The Journal, Appalachian Journal*, and *Pine Mountain Sand & Gravel*.

Anna Johnson Kline is a songwriter, musician, and poet. She is a Kentucky Arts Council Community Scholar and Performing Artist Directory musician, and Business Development Director for the International Bluegrass Music Association and co author of *Last Mule in the Holler*. *www.annaklinecreates.com*

Megan Krupa is the author of the chapbook, *Heirloom*. Her work has appeared in *BOAAT, Broad River Review*, and *Driftwood Press* among others. Her poems are deeply connected to place, rootedness, and community of Appalachia. She is an Assistant Professor at East Tennessee State University.

Originally from Radford, Virginia, **Lisa Kwong** is AppalAsian, an Affrilachian Poet, and author of *Becoming AppalAsian* (Glass Lyre Press), a finalist for the Weatherford Award in Poetry. Her poems have appeared in *Best New Poets, A Literary Field Guide to Southern Appalachia, Anthology of Appalachian Writers*, and other publications.

Chiquita Mullins Lee has won individual artist/excellence awards in creative writing from local and state arts councils and she performs and writes for local theater productions. Her poetry, fiction, and creative nonfiction are published nationally, and she co-authored the picture book *You Gotta Meet Mr. Pierce*, published by Kokila Press.

Cathy Cultice Lentes lives and writes in the Appalachian foothills near the Ohio River. She is the author of *Getting the Mail* (Finishing Line Press, 2016) and coauthor of *Stronger When We Touch* (The Orchard Street Press, 2023. Find out more at about her life and work at http://cathyculticelentes.com.

Tess Lloyd is a professor emerita at East Tennessee State University. She co-edited *Writing Appalachia: An Anthology* (2020) and is currently writing a quartet of novels about women, labor, slavery, and social reform in nineteenth-century New England and Appalachia.

Commonwealth University professor emerita **Marjorie Maddox** has published 16 poetry collections, *What She Was Saying* (stories), and 4 children's books. She is the assistant editor of *Presence*, and host of WPSU's *Poetry Moment*. She co-edited *Common Wealth: Contemporary Poets on Pennsylvania* and the forthcoming *Keystone* (PSU Press). www.marjoriemaddox.com

Jessica Manack is the author of *Gastromythology* (Sheila-Na-Gig Editions, 2024) and lives in Pittsburgh, Pennsylvania. Her work has recently appeared in *Still: The Journal, SWWIM Every Day*, and *Five South*, and has been nominated for the Pushcart Prize. Keep up with her at http://www.jessicamanack.com.

Karen Salyer McElmurray is the author of lyric essays, memoir and novels. *Wanting Radiance*, part mystery and part soul-journey is her most recent novel, from University Press of Kentucky. She recently published a collection of essays called *I Could Name God in Twelve Ways* in September 2024, also from UPK.

Jonie McIntire, Poet Laureate of Lucas County, Ohio, has authored three chapbooks, including *Semidomesticated*, (rereleased through Sheila-Na-Gig Editions in 2022) which won Red Flag Poetry's 2020 chapbook contest. She is poetry editor at *Of Rust and Glass*, Treasurer at Ohio Poetry Association and hosts Uncloistered Poetry from Toledo, Ohio.

Wendy McVicker is a former poet laureate of Athens, Ohio, and an Ohio Arts Council teaching artist. Her most recent book is a collaborative collection, *Stronger When We Touch* (The Orchard Street Press, 2023), and her chapbook from Sheila-Na-Gig Editions, is *Alone in the Burning*.

Barbara Marie Minney is an award-winning transgender poet and quiet activist. Barbara is the author of four collections: *If There's No Heaven, Poetic Memoir Chapbook Challenge, Dance Naked With God*, and *A Woman in Progress*. Barbara lives in Tallmadge, Ohio, with her wife of 43 years. Follow Barbara at www.barbaramarieminneypoetry.com.

Susan J. Mitchell has written four poetry books. Her latest is *Twice in a Lifetime* (2023). Her poetry has appeared in *Appalachian Journal, Appalachian Heritage* and others. She lives on a hilltop surrounded by hills and trees. She sits on her porch watching for deer, wild turkey, and rabbits.

Cathy Rigg Monetti is a writer and maker who heartily advocates the joys of living a creative life. Her work has appeared in *Litmosphere: Journal of Charlotte Lit; Still: The Journal;* and *Clinch Mountain Review.* Her short stories were finalists for the Doris Betts Fiction Prize (2023) and Lit/South (2023). cathyriggwriter.com

Laura Leigh Morris is the author of *The Stone Catchers: A Novel* (UP Kentucky, 2024) and *Jaws of Life: Stories* (West Virginia UP, 2018). She's previously published short fiction in *STORY Magazine, North American Review, Redivider, JMWW,* and other journals. She teaches creative writing and literature at Furman University in Greenville, SC. To learn more, visit www.lauraleighmorris.com.

Karen Whittington Nelson writes from her small Southeast Ohio farm. Her work has been published by *Women Speak, Sheila-Na-Gig Online, Main Street Rag, Gyroscope Review, Pine Mountain Sand & Gravel, Anthology of Appalachian Writers, Northern Appalachia Review, I Thought I Heard a Cardinal Sing: Ohio's Appalachian Voices,* and other journals.

Alexis T. Nichols is currently a student at Berea College, where she majors in English and minors in Creative Writing. She works as a writing consultant and spends her weekends where she grew up in Mercer County, Kentucky.

Miriam Nordine is passionate about supporting Ohio authors as the program coordinator at Ohioana Library. She is a writer and artist of various mediums, including collage, ceramics, painting and drawing. She is active in the Ohio arts community and loves spending time with her family. She is from Dover, Ohio.

Ali O'Rourke finally discovered what home felt like when, as a young adult, she moved to the forests and mountains of Appalachia. She's been a writer, teacher, caregiver, and seeker for at least a few lifetimes. Please contact her if you have any of this human thing figured out.

Elaine Fowler Palencia grew up in Morehead, KY, and Cookeville, TN. Her work has received eight Pushcart Prize nominations. She has published four poetry chapbooks, two collections of Appalachian short stories, a scholarly monograph on the Civil War, and four (fortunately) pseudonymous pulp novels.

Kaja S. Parker is a writer from Southwest Ohio. She has been a storyteller since grade school. She is currently a college student studying English and Creative Writing. When she isn't writing fiction, she's likely reading or listening to music. Find her at: parkerkaja04@gmail.com.

Lisa J. Parker is a native Virginian, a poet, musician, and photographer. Her first book, *This Gone Place*, won the 2010 Weatherford Award, her second book, *The Parting Glass*, won the 2021 Arthur Smith Poetry Prize, and she is widely published in literary journals. Her work may be found at www.wheatpark.com

Tina Parker is the author of the poetry collections *Lock Her Up*, *Mother May I*, and *Another Offering*. Tina grew up in Bristol, Virginia, and she is a long-time Kentucky resident. To learn more about her work, visit www.tina-parker.org or follow her on Instagram @tetched_poet.

Poet, playwright, essayist, and editor, **Linda Parsons** is the poetry editor for Madville Publishing and the copy editor for *Chapter 16*, the literary website of Humanities Tennessee. Her sixth collection, *Valediction*, contains poems and prose. Five of her plays have been produced by Flying Anvil Theatre in Knoxville, Tennessee.

Chrissie Anderson Peters lives in Bristol, TN, with her husband and feline children. She holds degrees from Emory & Henry College and the University of Tennessee. She has been published in *Still: The Journal*, *Women Speak*, and *Salvation South*, among others. Read more about her work at www.CAPWrites.com.

Sara Pisak is a reviewer, essayist, and poet. Sara recently published work in *The Rumpus*, *The Fourth River*, *Hippocampus*, *the Deaf Poets Society*, *Door = Jar*, and *Appalachian Journal*, among others. In total, she published over 100 pieces. When not writing, Sara spends time with her family and friends.

Sarah Pross was born, raised, and still resides in Seymour, Tennessee with her rescue pup Charley. She has a B.A. in English Literature from Maryville College, where she graduated in 2007. Her poetry has appeared in *Kakalak* and *Pine Mountain Sand & Gravel*. She is the author of *Grounding* (2021).

Bonnie Proudfoot's fiction, poetry, reviews, and essays appear in journals and anthologies, including *Women Speak*. Her novel, *Goshen Road* (2020) received WCONA's Book of the Year and was long-listed for the PEN/ Hemingway. Her poetry chapbook, *Household Gods*, can be found on Sheila-Na-Gig editions. Bonnie resides in Athens, Ohio.

Rita Sims Quillen's most recent poetry book, *Some Notes You Hold* (Madville 2020) has received a Bronze Medal from the Feathered Quill Book Awards, a finalist listing for poetry in the American Writing Awards and was a Bonus Book for the 2023 International Pulpwood Queens and Timber Guys Book Club. Her novel, *Wayland*, published by Iris Press in 2019, was the March 2022 Bonus Book of the Month for the International Pulpwood Queens and Timber Kings Book Club. Her poetry collection, *The Mad Farmer's Wife*, was a finalist for the Weatherford Award.

Amy Le Ann Richardson holds an MFA from Spalding University ('09). She is a farmer, writer, artist, and teacher and has received grants and fellowships from the Kentucky Foundation for Women. She is the author of *Who You Grow Into*, FLP 2024, and her work is featured in multiple journals.

Barbara Lyghtel Rohrer's work has appeared in *Women Speak (vol. 7)*; *I Thought I Heard the Cardinal Sing*; *Sun and Shadow, Wood and Stone*; *Bluestone Review*; *Geez*; and *The Sun*. Her site *The Invisible Map* (theinvisiblemap.com) explores through her writings and reflections of others what it means to listen within.

Born and raised in Carter County, Tennessee, **Rachel Rosolina** is Communications Director for Appalshop. A graduate of Berea College and West Virginia University, Rosolina has had work published in such outlets as *Still: The Journal*, *Women Speak*, *Untelling*, and *Belt Magazine*.

Leigh Claire Schmidli lives in the Bluegrass, where her colorful work history includes baker, barista, & custodian, complete with jangling keys. Recent writing can be found in *Nelle, Phoebe, & Ms. Aligned*, an anthology by women & non-binary authors—exploring who we choose to be and the visions that free us.

Roberta Schultz, author of *Asking Price* and *Underscore*, is a maker of songs, poems and drum circles. She writes some of her songs on a mountain in North Carolina, and is co-founder of the *Poet & Song Series* with her trio, Raison D'Etre. You can find out more at RobertaSchultz.com.

Lacy Snapp is a teacher and woodworker in East Tennessee. Her first chapbook, *Shadows on Wood*, was published in 2021. She is a MFA in Writing graduate of VCFA and holds an MA in English from ETSU where she is now a professor of literature and literary event planner.

Judith Sornberger lives on the side of the mountain in rural Tioga County, Pennsylvania. Her full-length poetry collections are: *Open Heart* (Calyx Books), *Practicing the World* (CavanKerry), *I Call to You from Time* (Wipf & Stock), and *Angel Chimes: Poems of Advent and Christmas*. www.judithsornberger.net

M. Lynne Squires is a Pushcart Prize-nominated author of four books, including the award winning *Letters to My Son, Reflections of Urban Appalachia at Mid-Century*. A poet and short story crafter, her work appears in numerous anthologies and journals including *Change Seven, The Ekphrastic Review*, and *Fearless: Women's Journeys to Self-Empowerment*.

A native of Hazard, Kentucky, **Tracy Staley** lives and works in Dayton, Ohio. Her writing has appeared in newspapers and magazines, most recently in *The Daily Yonder* and *Untelling* literary magazine. She works as a communications specialist for a Lexington, KY-based marketing agency, Great Stories LLC.

A Clermont County, Ohio native, **Sherry Cook Stanforth** founded Originary Arts Initiative, designing creative programming for diverse communities. She's managing editor of *Pine Mountain Sand & Gravel*, and a committed maker of river anthologies, fiction, poems, and albums. Her poetry collection *Drone String* is inspired by her mountain music heritage.

Natalie Sypolt lives and writes in North Central West Virginia. Her first book, *The Sound of Holding Your Breath*, was published by West Virginia University Press in 2018. Natalie currently is the writing coordinator at Pierpont Community & Technical College and teaches in the West Virginia Wesleyan Low-Residency MFA Program.

Jessica D. Thompson is the author of *Daybreak and Deep*—a finalist in the American Book Fest Best Books of 2022 for narrative poetry and she co-authored the children's book, *When Animals Miss the Sun*, (Brick Street Poetry). Her newest book, *The Mood Ring Diaries*, will be released in 2025.

Jacinda Townsend is the author of the forthcoming novel *Trigger Warning* (2025) and *Mother Country*, winner of the Ernest Gaines Award for Literary Excellence. Her first novel, *Saint Monkey*, won both the Janet Heidinger Kafka Prize and the James Fenimore Cooper Prize. Jacinda teaches at Brown University.

E. J. Wade's poems are published in *Women Speak, the New Ohio Review*, and *Salvation South*. A three-time Pushcart Award nominee, she holds a Doctor of Education from National Louis University, an MA from Shepherd University and an MA of Creative Media Practices from the University of The West of Scotland.

Kristi Stephens Walker is a freelance writer and editor from Charleston, WV. Her articles have appeared in local women's publications and magazines, and she has completed her first novel. Most recently, her poetry was selected for publication in the literary journal, *Untelling*. She lives in Nashville, TN.

Randi Ward is a poet, translator, lyricist, and photographer from Belleville, WV. She earned her MA in Cultural Studies from the University of the Faroe Islands and is a two-time recipient of the American-Scandinavian Foundation's Nadia Christensen Prize. Ward's work has been featured on Folk Radio UK, NPR, and PBS NewsHour. randiward.com/about/

Sharon Waters holds an MFA in Creative Writing from West Virginia Wesleyan College. Sharon has a play in the anthology, *30 Short Plays for Passionate Actors*, published by All Original Plays. She has also been published in *Longridge Review* and *MicroLit*. Sharon is currently at work on a memoir.

Violet Rae Webster is a singer/songwriter with ancestral ties to Pomeroy, Ohio, in Meigs County. She and sister, Roberta Schultz, have been performing for 34 years with the women's trio, Raison D'Etre, focusing on original songs plus different time periods of music with intricate three-part harmonies.

Donna Weems regularly sings at local festivals. She performed *I've Peas In My Pocket* with the Agusta Heritage Children's choir, is featured on the *Songs of Scott's Run* CD, joined Al Anderson, raising over $20,000 for Ugandan orphans and was a cast member of the folk operetta, *The Hobo's Homecoming*.

Laura Grace Weldon lives in a township too tiny for traffic lights where she works as a book editor, teaches writing workshops, serves as *Braided Way* editor, and chronically maxes out her library card. Laura was Ohio's 2019 Poet of the Year and is the author of four books.

Sherrell Runnion Wigal was born, raised and still lives in West Virginia. She writes from her rock-based road roots, with an eye and ear to women and a heart honed to the spirituality in life. To read Sherrell's poetry is to walk into a place we cannot always predict but is also somehow familiar. Her poems have appeared in many regional publications.

Dana Wildsmith is the author of *With Access to Tools*, from Madville Publishing and five other collections of poetry, a novel, *Jumping,* and an environmental memoir, *Back to Abnormal*, finalist for Georgia Author of the Year. She has served as Artist-in-Residence for Grand Canyon National Park and Everglades National Parks.

Kristine Williams lives and writes in Athens, OH, where she lives with her husband and is retired from teaching public speaking and interpersonal communication at a two-year college. She has grown children in Denver and Brooklyn.

Chris Wood manages numbers by day, spends most evenings cleaning up dog hair from the abundance of love from her fur-babies, and writes in between to balance her right brain from her left. Her work has appeared in several publications, including *Salvation South* and *Imspired*. Learn more at https://chriswoodwriter.com.

Karen Spears Zacharias is an American writer whose work focuses on women and justice. She holds an MA in Appalachian Studies from Shepherd University and an MA in Creative Media Practice from the University of West Scotland. She lives in Deschutes County, Oregon.

Acknowledgments

Goat-Footed Gods, (Carnegie Mellon): "Fairest of All,"
"Homegoing, West Virginia" and "Study on the Indigo Bunting"
OxMag: "Potato Poultice"
Still, The Journal: "Sawdust Meditations"
Sussurus: "All the Mothers"
Trigger Warning, (Graywolf): "Fences"
Untelling: "The Viewing"